Igor Ko

THE 3 LAWS OF
PSYCHOLOGY

Many experts view psychology as a preparadigmatic science at a primitive stage of development, lacking a consensus on human nature. However, very few people are aware of this perspective, and psychology scholars prefer not to acknowledge it. Perplexingly, psychology is a thriving field with a high demand for its services, all despite a very fragile theoretical foundation. This book introduces a new paradigm of psychology as a discipline rooted in physics and biology on the one hand and connected to philosophy on the other. Consequently, the structure of psychology is reconstructed on the basis of three postulates: - the law of preservation, the law of congregation, and the law of the universality of behavior. These laws shed light on fundamental questions of human existence: Why do we exist? What is the form of our existence? And how do we function? Important psychological subjects are reexamined, including the relationship between the body and mind, the categorization of human needs, the origin of human behavior, and the meaning of life. Subsequently, the developed novel perspective is used to investigate vital phenomena of the human soul, such as panic, depression, altruism, happiness, state of flow, midlife and other age-related crises, fear of death, and many others.

Contents

Introduction

Some years ago, I studied project management and execution. The fundamentals of this domain of knowledge begin with the description of the project phases, i.e., project definition, then followed by the appraisal, planning, implementation, and close-out. Numerous studies and thousands of books have been devoted to a thorough examination of this process. "Don't humans behave similarly?" I wondered as I examined this sequence of well-defined steps. "Don't we define our objectives, inform them, then plan and execute our daily activities in a similar pattern?" It sounded plausible because human actions are, in some ways, small projects. I was intrigued by this concept and attempted to conduct additional research. I assumed that the existing literature would be able to detail the main steps of human actions. Despite numerous searches, I was surprised to find none that provided a clear-cut unambiguous sequence of elements of human behavior.

Because I could not find any literature on the subject, I opted to outline a process diagram of human behavior myself (Kopsov, 2019a), which was the initial outcome of my ambitions. It soon became clear that establishing a schematic of the acting process essentially equated to conceptualizing an analytical model of human behavior, which sparked new ideas about other aspects of the human psyche. To begin with, the behavioral model led to the development of a theory of human happiness (Kopsov, 2019a), which in turn directed to a subject of satisfaction of needs and the subsequent establishment of an original model of human motivation (Kopsov, 2019b).

I also noticed that the process diagram of human behavior has an evolutionary perspective to it. I proposed that the principles of human behavior originate from a simple "action-reaction" type of response characterizing the matter, which transitions into a more complex need-governed functioning of biological organisms, and subsequently evolves into the process of human behavior (Kopsov, 2020b). Eventually, I realized that, in many cases, psychology, philosophy, and cosmogenesis are all part of the same body of knowledge. In that regard, I conceptualized a matrix system of evolution instead of the conventional linear view of it (Kopsov, 2021c). I then investigated the origins of human needs, redefined the classification of basic needs, and linked them to the primary laws of nature (Kopsov, 2021c).

The derived models of psychological phenomena were not a goal but an instrument for the pursuit of the resolution of fundamental questions of human existence, often entailing the fusion of psychology and philosophy. Through continuous development and alterations, devised postulations crystallized into a hypothesis of the three laws of psychology and philosophy.

The First Law is the Law of Preservation. This law defines the ultimate reason for the existence of human beings and the cosmos around us. It addresses the question: why do humans and the universe exist?

The Law of Congregation is the Second Law. This law defines the form of existence of human beings and the cosmos around us. It answers the question: how humans and the universe are arranged?

The Universal Law of Behavior is the third law. This law defines how humans and the universe function.

The theorized concepts enabled us to develop a new paradigm of psychology and define a unique perspective on the metaphysical development of the universe. We also apply postulated laws to some of life's most pressing questions: what is the meaning of life? What exactly is happiness, and how does one obtain it? What causes death fear? What is the relationship between the body and the mind? Why do people suffer from depression and panic? What are the major life stages, and how do they relate to age crises?

We unequivocally distinguish between the human mind and the human body as two distinct domains of human nature and unequivocally support the similarity of psychological processes in humans and nonhuman animals. We propose that inanimate matter, living organisms, and the conscious mind all behave in the same way. We extend evolutionary theory into the domain of the mind and reject the idea of culture/civilization as a separate stage of evolution. These ideas challenge many conventional views and may appear controversial.

Part One

It is Time for Psychology to Become a Normal Science

1   Modern Psychology - Flourishing but Primitive

Conventional psychology has largely abandoned efforts to resolve the fundamental matters of the human psyche in favor of focusing on the peculiarities of human behavior. This is exemplified by the fragmentation of psychological schools, their failure to define a standard paradigm, and a widely spread incapability to produce verifiable psychological research. Because of its inability to depart from descriptive approaches, modern psychology should be classed as a "branch of knowledge" rather than a science. This viewpoint may surprise many and sound demeaning to psychology professionals. Although the American Psychological Association's official website (American Psychological Association [APA], n.d.) states that "psychology has been considered a preparadigmatic science by many theorists, in contrast to physics and chemistry (regarded as normal sciences)."

Further, it defines preparadigmatic science as "a science at a primitive stage of development, before it has achieved a paradigm and established a consensus about the true nature of the subject matter and how to approach it." This notion has been echoed throughout centuries by many prominent scholars. Hergenhahn (2008), in *An Introduction to the History of Psychology*, suggests that the "closest psychology ever came to being a single-paradigm discipline was during the Middle Ages when departures from the view of humans contained in church dogma were simply not tolerated." He further outlines a timeline of quotes made by prominent scholars, which follows the psychology discipline's formation over more than 200 years.

In the eighteenth century, a philosopher, Immanuel Kant (1786), wrote the following regarding the place of psychology within the domain of science - "the empirical doctrine of the soul ... must remain even further .... from the rank of what may be called a natural science proper" (*Preface* 471).

Just over a hundred years later, William James (1892), the "father of American psychology," described psychology as:

> A string of raw facts; a little gossip and a wrangle about opinions; a little classification and generalization on the mere descriptive level; a strong prejudice that we have states of mind, and that our brain conditions them: but not a single law in the same sense in which physics shows us laws, not a single proposition from which any consequence can causally be deduced.... This is no science, it is only the hope for a science. (p. 335)

In the mid-twentieth century, American philosopher and psychologist Edna Frances Heidbreder (1933) made the following reflection:

> For psychology is a science that has not yet made its great discovery. It has found nothing that does for it what atomic theory has done for chemistry, the principle of organic evolution for biology, the laws of motion for physics. Nothing that gives it a unifying principle has yet been discovered or recognized. (pp. 425–426)

Recently, a psychologist and philosopher, Sigmund Koch (1993), described the discipline as psychological studies rather than as the science of psychology:

> Psychology is misconceived when seen as a coherent science or as any kind of coherent discipline devoted to the empirical study of human beings. Psychology, in my view, is not a single discipline but a collection of studies of varied cast, some few of which may qualify as science, whereas most do not. (p. 902)

These century-spanning reflections on the scientific status of psychology help shed light on the progress – or lack of it – of establishing a unified paradigm of psychology.

Since its conception, psychology has mainly existed within the confines of social sciences. There were periods in the twentieth century when psychology stood at the crossroads of embracing the rules of natural sciences. However, the temptation of the scientific method was never enough to outweigh the influence of the orthodoxy of the humanistic-centered view. Despite the many theses written on methodologies in psychology, the primary method of psychologists remains self-assessment. The problem of psychology is not that it resides in a "preparadigmatic state" – but rather that its current practicing experts lack the natural and applied science mindset. They continue to replicate and reproduce their existing attitude to batches of fresh graduates emerging in great numbers from universities worldwide. No wonder it took the superstar physicist Stephen Hawking (1988), and not a psychologist, to raise the key challenge of modern psychological research: how to predict human behavior from mathematical equations?

Debate on the unified paradigm of psychology – which had attracted a lot of interest for some time – has been pushed to the fringes of scientific discourse, and an ever-increasing number of schools of psychological thought and psychotherapy continue to emerge. According to John Norcross, a Professor of Psychology at the University of Scranton, there are now at least 500 types of psychotherapies (Lilienfeld & Arkowitz, 2012). At the same time, Wampold (2001), Professor of Counseling Psychology at the University of Wisconsin–Madison, concluded that the employed therapy school accounts for only about one percent of therapeutic effectiveness. The scientific paradigm has little significance for people who use psychological therapies. Belonging to a particular school of psychology is likewise losing relevance inside academic circles. These observations lead to the very reasonable question of why a single paradigm for psychology is even necessary.

People in contemporary society struggle with anxiety as "family values," conventional social ties, and the role of religion all continue to deteriorate. In this scenario, psychotherapists increasingly take on the role of an hourly-paid priest, friend, or relative. Even in its current state, psychology continues to attract clients and consumers seeking psychological support as well as a sense of belonging and self-realization. It may be claimed that psychology is in a good place right now. The number of psychologists in the United States alone is currently close to 180,000 (Bureau of Labor Statistics, 2022) and is projected to increase by 8% from 2020 to 2030. This growth can be anticipated to be considerably faster for the rest of the world as low- and middle-income nations continue to close the social and economic gap with high-income countries. If the per capita coverage in the United States were applied globally, there would be 4.3 million psychologists.

One can reasonably conclude that the commercial prospects of psychology have never looked brighter - even though the discipline has suffered from decades of insufficient

15

scientific development. As a result, the situation is somewhat peculiar: psychology is experiencing increasing commercial success, growing public attention, and at the same time, scientific stagnation. Regarding the latter, it appears that psychology is not only moving from one crisis to the next but also building up these crises: the never-ending search for a common paradigm, the absence of any sort of unified theory, and a relatively recent crisis involving the inability to replicate results as a sizable portion of psychological research is unable to replicate the findings of the earlier studies (Diener & Biswas-Diener, 2020). We believe that these crises are just various manifestations of the same fundamental problem.

2   Towards a Miracle of the Unified Psychology

Psychology is a deeply divided branch of knowledge. Textbooks routinely refer to anything from five to eight major perspectives, the most common being behavioral, biological, cognitive, humanistic, psychoanalytical, and social. On the one hand, these classifications allow placing the development of psychology in a historical context. On the other hand, they attempt to categorize the leading schools of thought. Such taxonomies are inevitably inadequate as psychology is a very loosely arranged discipline without a coherent framework that could have allowed it to construct a robust body of science. In this regard, the merit of establishing a unified psychology theory is much broader than it may appear at first. It would mark the formation of a paradigm of psychological studies, thus, enabling their long-overdue transformation into the ranks of a 'proper science.' In essence, the concepts of unified psychology and the paradigm of psychology are the same. The development of the unified theory concerns the collective status of psychology and the personal reputation of its practitioners and scholars.

It is rather symptomatic that the pursuit for unification split into multiple camps and schools of thought, in particular, unified psychology and unified psychotherapy.

Unified psychotherapy became a well-organized movement under the umbrella of the Society for the Exploration of Psychotherapy Integration (SEPI). *The Handbook of Psychotherapy Integration* was published in 2003 and has undergone several editions. Its second edition by Norcross & Goldfried (2005) recognizes four general integration routes of psychotherapy: common factors, technical eclecticism, theoretical integration, and assimilative integration. There are also hybrid approaches, as some of these routes may overlap, particularly theoretical and assimilative integration concepts. Norcross (2005) summarized the key factors obstructing psychotherapy unification as (1) partisan zealotry, (2) inadequate training, (3) fundamental differences in epistemology and ontology, (4) the lack of a common language, and (5) the challenge of continually expanding elements that need to be incorporated. However, we question the extent to which unified psychotherapy is credible without unified psychology, as having the former without the latter equates to developing treatments for disorders without fully grasping their underlying fundamental causes.

In comparison to psychotherapy, the unification of psychology is less structured. In the early days, ideas for its unification manifested through the unilateral claims for virtuousness by proponents of certain dominant schools,

17

particularly Behaviorism. Today, the division into schools has largely faded; instead, eclecticism prevails. Nevertheless, individual scholars continue to undertake efforts toward unification. Wilson (1998) attempted to reconcile differences within psychology within the framework of evolutionary theory. Concepts of unification were also emerging from neighboring branches of knowledge, as exemplified by Wilber's (2001) *Theory of Everything*. The journal of *The Review of General Psychology* dedicated a special issue to unified psychology in 2013.

Henriques (2011) took a step toward unified psychology and presented its comprehensive theory, which consisted of four "pieces that combine to provide a new framework for understanding human behavior and the human condition:" (1) Behavioral Investment Theory, (2) the Influence Matrix, (3) the Justification Hypothesis, and (4) the Tree of Knowledge System. Henriques' (2011) unified theory brings an original approach to many aspects of psychology and offers an intriguing perspective on many issues. However, the generalist character of the concept complicates its further dissemination, as fellow scholars are required to accept a somewhat compounded theoretical apparatus with limited empirical sense (Hayes, 2004).

The general integration routes and corresponding hindrances in the development of unified psychology are the same as in the case of psychotherapy. However, we would like to emphasize two additional underlying obstacles. The first is the resignation of the scientific community on the matter and its tacit acceptance of the status quo, fed by inertia and reproduced over many generations by a university system deep-rooted in the tradition of social (and not natural) science.

The other factor contributing to the stagnation of psychology as a science is, somewhat paradoxically, its commercial success. The progress of any science is first determined by the demand from economic sectors and society in general. Society at large is content with the services provided by psychology professionals, as they have successfully filled the vacuum left by the retreat of religion, the demise of "family values," and the disintegration of traditional communities. In the case of psychology, there are no critical extrinsic factors driving progress, in contrast to the situation with applied, natural, and some other social sciences. Moreover, psychologists are often responsible for defining the objectives, methods, as well as success criteria of their work.

A movement toward the unification of psychology is separated into two opposing camps: the supporters of the "natural science model" of unified psychology and their opponents representing the "eclectics" camp.

Kimble (1996) summarized the views of proponents of the natural science perspective. According to him, the unified psychology:

> ...portrays psychology as a natural science and offers a set of axioms, fashioned after Newton's laws of motion, as the fundamental principles that hold the field together. The argument begins with a reminder that a science of psychology must obey the rules of science: it must be deterministic, empirical, and analytic. To honor those criteria, it must be some form of behaviorism, based on stimuli and response. (p. ix)

Echoing these views, renowned physicist Stephen Hawking (1988) predicted that mathematical equations would describe human behavior. While Green (2015) offered a more nuanced outline of a roadmap to the unification of psychology by advocating the use of "more neutral, and ... more rigorous (e.g., formal) terms:"

> What is required from a unification proposal is a theory, probably framed in a mathematical or otherwise formal language, which rigorously captures apparently disparate phenomena. The chief reasons to employ a formal language are essentially threefold. First, a formal language can bridge across areas that differ in terms of their concrete content, but that have similar underlying structural properties. Second, it is in formal languages that the work of prediction, and the sort of explanation that relies upon prediction, can be most satisfactorily achieved. ... accurate prediction of new phenomena is certainly an impressive achievement when it can be attained, and it is most convincingly accomplished in the context of a formal language. ... Finally, formal languages often have the ability to short-circuit the all-too-common impulse to become mired in endless (and often pointless) a priori disputes about which theoretical ideology is to be preferred – for example, behavioral, evolutionary, humanistic, and so forth. If the predictions work, they work. (p. 208)

Advocates of eclecticism and postmodernism contest the natural science model of unified psychology and instead promote the amalgamation of diverse schools of thought (Sternberg & Grigorenko, 2001):

Under this approach, an individual ... [must] study the phenomena of interest from multiple points of view. The individual thus would reach a fuller understanding of the phenomena being studied because he or she would not be limited by a set of assumptions or methods drawn from only one field of psychology. (p. 1075)

Intriguingly, the conceptualists of unified psychology are not confident in the success of the mission, evaluating its chances with relatively subdued optimism. According to Green (2015), pursuing unification is not just an attempt "for unification, but for a unificatory miracle:"

Principles of unification, whatever they might be, would seem to require, at minimum, a relatively stable set of concepts (and objects) in order to do their work. But so much in psychology remains highly malleable that it is hard to see how principles could be formed to rigorously capture them when their meanings might change by the time of the next textbook edition. Is it possible that principles of unification would play a significant role in stabilizing the network of psychological concepts objects? Yes, it is possible, but now we are asking that a unification we do not yet understand do something we aren't able to do for ourselves. (p. 212)

We do not share this skepticism and endeavor to demonstrate that applying the schematic of human behavior for the unification of the divided perspectives not only implements Green's vision but finds an amicable compromise between the contesting concepts of psychology unification.

In the early stages, we intentionally concentrated on a model rather than a theory of unified psychology (Kopsov, 2021b) due to the firm belief that any theory requires a foundation of analytical modeling. Furthermore, it was hardly plausible to make a claim for a universal theory within the confines of a single paper. Further, we address multiple issues of the human psyche in a structured manner by providing an analytical model for each analyzed aspect of the human mind and behavior. In this way, we claim to offer a novel paradigm and a unified theory of psychology. Although it is a first incremental step, the formation of genuinely unified psychology is a process rather than a statement, as it requires acceptance and commitment from scholars representing various schools of thought.

3   Psychology 1.0 - Application of Analytical Modeling

A "proper" science does not confine itself to observations but uncovers the underlying drivers of the phenomenon in question, converts these into analytical models, and concentrates on quantitative assessments and predictions. Analytical modeling provides the basis for the many successes of engineering disciplines and natural sciences. Only when an analytical model is in place can researchers, doctors, and engineers conduct their work in a professional and unspeculative manner. Analytical models do not "exist per se;" they are products of analytical thinking and manifest the essential features of the subject of examination. They structure the acquired knowledge and allow us to focus research or design in an optimal direction – none of which is possible in contemporary psychology.

When doctors do their job, for example, conducting a medical checkup, the very first thing they do is to select an appropriate examination method, of which they have many. They can check body temperature, oxygen saturation, blood pressure, pulse, respiratory rate, and many other parameters. They can opt for more complex examinations, e.g., blood testing, biopsy, or magnetic resonance imaging. In most instances, the characteristics they measure (oxygen saturation, cholesterol level, blood pressure, etc.) are meaningful only if studied within a specific analytical model of human body functioning, of which there are many. These can be integral models of the body (e.g., mechanical, biochemical), models of systems (e.g., cardiovascular, digestive), organs (e.g., liver, heart), or cells. Each model contains a definition of its purpose, application limits, system description, methods for examination, acceptance criteria, failure moods, measurable parameters, etc.

When psychologists attempt to check that a human psyche is in good condition, they have nothing of this kind at their disposal, nothing to measure, no properties to define, and no criteria to comply with. For example, if psychologists attempt to analyze human emotions, all they have at their disposal is a set of descriptive concepts, often with contrasting views. If it were validation of physical health, it would be equivalent to a doctor saying that a patient is fine because they had seen people in similar conditions doing well. Psychologists justify the absence of analytical modeling by the complexity of the human psyche, implying that other activities, like designing a spacecraft or performing brain surgery, are more manageable tasks. We do not subscribe to this point of view and instead attribute it to the legacy of theological doctrines of the soul, which saw human nature as a product of divine creation, which shall not be studied but observed.

Renowned philosopher Immanuel Kant long ago addressed the failure of psychology to establish itself as a proper science. He rebelled against religious views on science by proclaiming that "a doctrine of nature can only contain so much science proper as there is in it of applied mathematics," (Kant, 1786, *Preface* 470). However, he succumbed to orthodox thinking regarding psychology by admitting that "the empirical doctrine of the soul ... must remain even further ... from the rank of what may be called a natural science proper" (*Preface* 471). Kant (1786) defined analytical modeling (construction of mathematical conceptions in his words) as a foundation of proper science, but (unfortunately), he did not see how it is possible to apply analytical modeling to psychology. By the way, he erroneously claimed that analytical modeling could not be used in chemistry either. Unlike psychologists, the chemists did not yield to the constraints imposed on them but claimed their science by fully embracing analytical modeling and making it a success story. Kant is not to blame for the misfortunes of psychology. He did not define or curse its destiny but provided his reflections (turned prophecy) at the time when theological doctrines were still dominant.

It is not the complexity of the subject but the lack of method that fails psychology. Unfortunately, its search for a method follows the steps of alchemy rather than a "proper science" chemistry. One may wonder why psychology defied analytical modeling as its method. Some answers are on the surface: inability to shrug the theological origin of the concept of the psyche; flawed educational system; affluent and continuously growing customer base; self-complacency among scholars; lack of economic incentives and competitiveness among psychology professionals (Kopsov, 2020a). However, the genuinely perplexing question is how did psychology manage *not* to adopt analytical modeling? The probability of this happening appears to be minuscule, considering that there were, and still are, many factors that favor the introduction of analytical modeling.

Psychology is usually taught at universities where other sciences embracing analytical modeling are studied. How did psychology fence itself from the influence of these sciences for several centuries? Why did some researchers not "defect" from the traditional orthodox thinking, especially considering that analytical modeling is a "low-hanging fruit" potentially bringing an abundance of benefits? How could, through all this time, psychology was not introduced to analytical modeling as a result of some accidental occurrence? The mystery remains to be uncovered by the future generation of psychologists.

In our recent works, we proposed analytical models of multiple psychological phenomena (Kopsov, 2019a, 2019b, 2020b, 2021c). Together, they form a structured and comprehensive theory of psychology integrated with other branches of science. They, in essence, represent a new paradigm that goes beyond the psychology field and provides a broader perspective of cosmogenesis. This realization is noteworthy, considering that, thus far, conventional psychology has failed to produce even a basic set of postulates. Contemporary psychology stays in the shadow of technological progress, which has sustained centuries of continuous advancements and is now entering its fourth phase or era commonly referred to as the Fourth Industrial Revolution or "Industry 4.0". Optimistically, this essay should contribute to transforming psychological research to the rank of proper science and the emergence of the first psychological doctrine, "Psychology 1.0".

Part Two

The First Law of Psychology –
The Law of Preservation

4   Why do Humans and the Universe Exist?

Since the times of Aristotle, people have distinguished between specific categories of nature. Aristotle's theory of hierarchical organization ranked all organisms, from plants to animals, to human beings, in a system where those at successively higher levels had all of the properties of those of lower levels and additional ones as well. Seeing the world as consisting of different levels of complexity is fundamental to many branches of science. For instance, Sellars (1926) identified these levels as inanimate matter, animate nature, mind, and society/persons/civilization. Henriques and colleagues (Henriques, 2003; Henriques & Michalski, 2019; Henriques et al., 2019) echo such views and advocate "universal behaviorism." A concept that characterizes the universe as an unfolding wave of hierarchically arranged dimensions of behavioral complexity – Matter, Life, Mind, and Culture. Within this classification, each behavioral act of a higher dimension of complexity is consequent to the functioning of lower dimensions. From this vantage point, behavior is the primary function of existence or, in a broader sense, is the existence itself.

The scientific discourse concerning distinct ontological levels of organization of living systems is far from over (Kirchhoff & Froese, 2017). We will elaborate on this subject later, but first, we would like to focus on analyzing the fundamental reasons for behavior, particularly the behavior of matter, life, and mind.

Humans incorporate multiple categories of nature, i.e., matter (physical substance), body (living organism), and mind

28

(consciousness). In this capacity, they represent the most appropriate object for analyzing the primary laws of the universe's existence. As a congregation of physical substances, humans are unequivocally part of the physical world and are subject to material forces and their effects (such as the act of falling due to the effect of forces of gravity). The materials of our bodies are subject to all laws governing the existence of inanimate matter, the main ones being the laws of conservation of mass and energy, which are essential postulates within the overall doctrine of the universe. Nevertheless, these laws play a trivial role in forming the human psyche, and their impact is most evident in how they affect physiological functions.

As biological beings, humans comply with the basic principles governing the existence of living organisms which were first formulated by "naturalist" scholars in the late eighteenth and nineteenth centuries. In *An Essay on the Principle of Population*, Malthus (1798) coined the notion of "struggle for existence," which originated from the hypothesis that living organisms exist in numbers far greater than can survive and reproduce. This excess of organisms is required to ensure the prosperity of a group by enhancing its robustness. It safeguards against the demise of some individuals and fosters internal competition as one of the driving forces behind group success. In the consequently conceived theory of natural selection developed by Darwin (1859) and Wallace (1858), any organism's primary tasks are self-preservation and reproduction. In combination, these two drives translate into the principle of preservation of organisms and their groups.

Darwin's theory of natural selection of organisms defines an overall vector of evolution as a process of enhancement of the individual's ability to compete, survive, and reproduce. It represents one of the dominant paradigms of biology as well as the overall concept of nature at large. Its introduction had a revolutionary impact on a vast range of natural and social sciences. Nevertheless, the theory is deeply rooted in biology, i.e., the scientific study of the life of organisms that are made up of cells and process genetic information encoded in genes. Unequivocally, the general laws of natural history and biology apply to humans, at least in their capacity as biological beings. However, an individual has a dual nature comprising a biological body and a conscious mind. In this regard, Darwin's theory does not allow a complete comprehension of human existence as it is ambiguous on the issue of interrelation between body and mind.

On the one hand, it provides a plausible viewpoint on how the mind may cater to enhancing abilities to compete, survive, and reproduce. On the other hand, regarding the mind's functionality, Darwin's (1859) theory's applicability is limited. It is hardly suited for conceptualizing phenomena based not on genetic encoding but on neuronal and symbolic information processing.

From a biological perspective, not much happened in the evolution of humankind over the last 2000-3000 centuries of ancestry development. Rutherford (2020) observed it rather wittingly:

> If you tidied up a Homo sapiens woman or man from 200,000 years ago, gave them a haircut, and dressed them in twenty-first-century clothes, they would not look out of place in any city in the world today. There's a conundrum in that stasis. Though we may not look different, humans did change, and profoundly. There's debate about when this transition

occurred, but by 45,000 years ago, something had happened. Many scientists think that it was a sudden change— sudden in evolutionary terms means hundreds of generations and dozens of centuries, rather than a thunderbolt. We don't quite have the language to relate to the timescales involved in such transitions. But what we can observe from the archaeological record is that we see the emergence and accumulation of a number of behaviors that are associated with modern humans, and there was a time before that where we see fewer or none of them. Given how long life has existed on Earth, this switch happened relatively in a heartbeat. The transformation occurred not in our bodies or physiology or even in our DNA. What changed was culture. (pp. 3-4)

Darwin's theory is irrelevant to the description of the mind and culture-driven phenomena. It needs to be complemented by a concept that addresses the evolution of modern humankind in its entirety. In this regard, we hypothesize that the dedicated law of preservation must also govern the domain of the mind, but – if there is such a law of preservation of the mind – unlike with matter and body, it is not fully transparent how it is exemplified. Hence, further, we attempt to shed some light on this subject.

Building on analogies with matter and life, we put forward the notion that the law of preservation of the mind is exemplified by the preservation and reproduction of cognitive information, which is achieved through its dissemination and absorption. The mind concerns the mental aspect of existence and comprises mental images of the world, encapsulating conscious, subconscious, imaginative, intelligent, judgmental,

31

perceptional, and linguistic perspectives. In a broader view, the definition of the mind also includes personal skills, capabilities, memories, views, and cognitive interactions with the world. The common attribute of all characteristics of the mind is cognitive information; therefore, at its very essence, the sole function of the mind is to process cognitive information, which is also the key enabler of social processes. In a civilizational context, the exchange of information enables education and empowerment of individuals, the exchange of knowledge between members of society, and the preservation of norms (whether social, economic, scientific, or ethical), as well as the continuation of regulations and traditions.

In line with Malthus' (1798) proposition that organisms exist in numbers far greater than can successfully reproduce, which results in the so-called "struggle for existence," we postulate that humans also produce far more cognitive information than can ever be exchanged and accumulated between and by individuals. This notion results in what we refer to as the "struggle for informational distribution." An excess of cognitive information is required to ensure the informational prosperity of both any single individual and of groups, as its shortage would result in insufficient knowledge and skills. As Darwin (1859) and Wallace (1858) developed the theory of "natural selection," we put forward the notion of *"informational selection,"* – according to which the fundamental determinations of mental existence are the preservation and reproduction of cognitive information, which are enabled through its dissemination and absorption. These features exemplify the principle of preservation of the mind when relating to individuals and their groups.

Figure 1. The law of preservation.

In summary, we advance the theory that the most fundamental law of nature is the law of preservation, which ultimately governs the universe's existence, and from which all other laws of physics, mechanics, chemistry, biology, and other sciences originate. In each phase of evolutionary development, the law of preservation manifests itself through a more elaborate formulation. First is the preservation of matter, then the preservation of life, and finally, the preservation of the mind (Figure 1). These three laws of preservation fuse together the principles of the existence of separate domains of human life. The law of preservation is the ultimate reason all processes in nature occur.

The law of preservation reveals itself through our instincts and is reflected in philosophical and ethical doctrines and habitual features of human living. Consider, for example, a fear of death. We take our desire to live for granted; it is innate to us and cast in moral and religious doctrines. But where does this instinct come from? The answer is that our desire to live is an effect of the universal law of preservation, and more specifically – preservation of life and mind.

The origin of the law of preservation remains a mystery. Controversially, one may argue that life and the universe's existence generally do not make sense. Why does matter exist? Why electrons and protons do not collide and vanish by negating each other? Why do male mammals risk their well-being in deadly fights to get the upper hand in sexual breading, while females risk theirs in defending outsprints? Why are humans prepared to endure psychological and physiological pain rather than end encountered suffering by ending their lives? Why bother about anything? Life and the universe's existence also do not make sense because they defy entropy principles, i.e., the general strive for disorder. The second law of thermodynamics states that an isolated system's entropy (disorder) never decreases in large systems over significant periods. This principle implies that the universe shall strive for uniformity, and any variations and peculiarities represented by any unique arrangements of matter (e.g., substances), life (e.g., organisms), or mind (e.g., human minds) shall cease to exist. However, the referred law is valid only for the so-called enclosed system, which is often illustrated by a distribution of weightless gas atoms or molecules inside an enclosed box. With time, all gas particles will become uniformly distributed within the box's volume. However, this will not happen if the system is not enclosed and affected from the outside. For example, if there is a hole on a side or the box is unevenly heated, the particles will never have a uniform distribution and continuously establish unique arrangements. Since entropy can increase in an open system, this may indicate that the universe is an open system, i.e., it is exposed to some outside influence, which manifests itself through the law of preservation, effected through a comprehensive need for the existence of matter, life, and mind.

One may argue that the laws of preservation act not only on an individual but also on a group level, and groups strive for their preservation as well. From this vantage point, assistance expedited by humans to each other represents a manifestation of the law of preservation. Thus, an altruistic desire to help others is not only a display of moral principles but a demonstration of the laws of nature.

Part Three

The Four Basic Human Needs

5   Needs of the Body and the Mind

Many motivation theories attempt to derive a taxonomy of human needs. Perhaps, the most publicly renowned scholar on the subject, Maslow (1943b), initially contemplated a five-level system comprising needs for safety, belonging, love, esteem, and self-actualization. He subsequently extended it to seven levels by adding cognitive and aesthetic needs (Maslow, 1970a), and then to eight levels by including transcendence needs (Maslow, 1970b).

Alderfer (1969) compressed Maslow's classification to the three so-called ERG needs - existence, relatedness, and growth. Similarly, McClelland (1988) also conceived three key driving motivators but defined these as needs for achievement, affiliation, and power. Reiss (2004) expanded the list to 16 basic desires. That was still less than the earlier system by Murray (1938), which consisted of primary needs based upon biological demands and 22 psychological needs, which were not fundamental for basic survival but essential for psychological well-being.

Many theories attempt to classify human needs, but none have gained general acceptance. They all share common deficiencies: (1) they are all intuitive, mainly aimed at composing systems suiting the observed pattern of human behavior and expressed in layman's terminology; (2) they fail to distinguish needs that are vital for the survival of individuals and the human species in general; and (3) they mostly fail to capitalize on the body of knowledge generated within natural sciences.

To rectify these drawbacks, we propose a novel theory of motivation by firmly linking the basic needs to the dominant traits of biological and mental existence. We conceive that human needs originate from the fundamental laws of functioning of body and mind and, first, from the laws of preservation. In this capacity, needs transform the generic principles of biological and mental nature into motivational mechanisms of human behavior. Accordingly, we postulate that laws of preservation of the human body and mind translate into the four basic human needs: (1) self-preservation, (2) reproduction, (3) absorption of information, and (4) dissemination of information. The former two needs predominantly define the functioning of the body, while the latter two needs predominantly define the functioning of the mind. Absorption and dissemination of cognitive information can also be seen as the preservation and reproduction of information.

Despite their different origins, the four basic needs are intrinsically interlinked. For example, the exchange of information is not only a cognitive function but also plays a role in reproduction, as the latter involves the exchange of genetically encoded information. Similarly, human reproduction contains a significant cognitive component, exemplified by the substantive teaching children receive in their formative years, as parenting implies fostering intelligence and social adaptation. Consider also how cognitive information enhances self-preservation when knowledge becomes an instrument of continued survival. The fusion of body and mind causes many similar cases of the interconnection of basic needs. Nevertheless, the four basic needs remain very distinct due to their different origins, and their interactions can be symbiotic or contesting.

39

The human psyche is affected by conflicting priorities of basic needs and existential conflicts between the mind and the body, and between the individual and society. Consequently, individuals exist within an ever-changing inner state and fluid extrinsic circumstances, resulting in the highly complex character of the human psyche. The contradictory and dynamic nature of human motivation is best explained by the ring model of human needs (Kopsov, 2019b), in which distinct needs are illustrated as rings within an overall circle of motives. The model allows for analyzing the dynamics of human needs from momentary, ontogenetic, or evolutionary perspectives.

In the momentary perspective, all distinct needs compete for an individual's "attention" within the ever-changing setting a person finds themself in, as distinct needs appear, disappear, are satisfied, or negated. For example, consider a feeling of hunger triggering the emergence of a need for sustenance while its subsequent satisfaction diminishes this particular need once again. This highly fluid state of needs is depicted by the dynamic ring model (Figure 2b), which is well-suited for modeling "distinct needs," i.e., transiently experienced components of the human psyche, including wants, desires, and wishes. The more dominant a distinct need is, the larger its associated ring and the closer it is to the exterior of the circle of needs. As a need gets satisfied, its dominance decays and the diameter of the corresponding ring reduces.

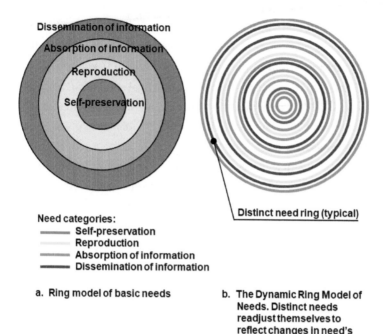

Need categories:
―――― Self-preservation
―――― Reproduction
―――― Absorption of information
―――― Dissemination of information

a. Ring model of basic needs

b. The Dynamic Ring Model of Needs. Distinct needs readjust themselves to reflect changes in need's dominance.

Figure 2. A ring model of human needs.

Ontogenetic and evolutionary perspectives of human needs are better depicted by the general ring model. For example, Figure 2a illustrates a typical ring model of basic needs. Within this model, a dedicated ring is allocated to each need, and its size (area) corresponds to a need's dominancy or "relative weight." A novelty of this model is that it enables the introduction of quantitative methods to trace the evolvement of needs within the context of a life span and the evolutionary progression.

The four basic needs are not just "intuitively suggested" through observations of human activity but methodologically derived from widely accepted or newly hypothesized laws of the preservation of organisms and the mind. Therefore, it is not by accident that they are well suited for quantitative assessment, as they can be matched with measurable parameters. Examples include levels of adrenaline or metabolism as quantifiable parameters of the need for self-preservation; levels of testosterone as a measurable parameter of the need for reproduction; kilobits of information received as a quantifiable parameter for the need for information absorption, and kilobits of information shared as a measurable parameter of the need for information dissimilation. The breadth of such possible measurable parameters is so vast that they can be precisely selected to suit the evaluation of particular factors of human life. Most extant taxonomies of needs (e.g., Maslow, 1943b; McClelland, 1988; Reiss, 2004) are unsuitable for quantification, as it is impossible to conceive a measurable parameter (apart from the unreliable and unstandardized method of self-assessment) associated with them, as there are no systems that allow for grading such things as needs for love, power, social belonging, etc.

The four proposed basic needs correlate to an extent with traditional "layman" classifications of needs and definitions used by conventional theories of motivation. In this regard, the basic need for self-preservation equates to a combination of what is commonly defined as physiological needs (except for sex) and safety needs. The basic reproduction need includes sex, child-rearing, and intrasexual dominance. The basic need to absorb information manifests itself through learning, acquisition of skills, social belonging, imitation, and conformity with social traditions. The basic need for dissemination of information correlates with aspirations for respect, ego, status, child mental upbringing, mastery, and competency, as these are characteristics and abilities which

42

allow individuals to command attention and spread their views. Moreover, many traditionally defined needs (e.g., needs for belonging, self-actualization, etc.) represent narrative – rather than analytical – descriptions of the "inner-self," as a majority of these are multi-componential and relate to more than just a single basic need.

Additionally, some commonly recognized basic needs fall outside our proposed taxonomy of basic needs, such as the need for friendship (Maslow, 1943b). According to our classification of motives, friendship does not represent a basic need, but a social instrument for self-preservation as well as the absorption and dissemination of cognitive information. The absence of friends is not detrimental to one's existence. However, they provide a safety cushion, a social network, means of access to essential information, and a community for sharing one's ideas and views.

One verification criterion for distinguishing basic needs from other needs is if a basic need is not collectively satisfied, it results in the extinction of a species within one generation. The four basic needs fully meet this criterion, as an inability to fulfill any of them would result in the termination of the existence of a being or its direct descendants. Conversely, desires for esteem, love, and self-actualization do not fit this verification criterion, even though they are evident in the realms of desires and wishes, and their satisfaction affects subjective well-being and quality of life. Based on these considerations, a basic need can be defined as a need upon which the survival of a species is conditional. Unlike prevailing theories of motivation, which represent either intuitive or mental constructs, the postulated taxonomy of needs is closely integrated with biology and social science concepts. The basic needs are elementary, i.e., not composed of other needs, while all other needs originate from them.

Precise identification of basic needs is vital, not only within the context of psychological studies but also for a broader range of social sciences and disciplines, including anthropology, communication science, political science, law, etc. Take as an example practice of legal sentencing to solitary confinement and the ongoing discourse on whether it is a cruel punishment. Solitary imprisonment is still applied despite some legal professionals considering that it is dehumanizing "as it deprives people of their biological needs, drastically changes their physiology and causes severe psychological and physical harm"(Coppola, 2019, p. 225). Our theory of basic human needs provides unambiguous support for the latter viewpoint. Being in captivity diminishes both the selection of needs that can be contemplated and the extent of their possible gratification. However, individuals, in many instances, are still able to experience the attainment of most of the four basic needs, albeit to a significantly reduced extent. In the case of solitary confinement, the situation is dramatically different as an individual is denied the possibility to cater to three of the four basic needs, particularly the needs for reproduction, information absorption, and information dissemination. This type of incarceration, whilst allowing for the existence of the body, imposes particularly dire conditions on the functioning of the mind, which is dependent on the exchange of cognitive information. Effectively, this means that the environment for the continued survival of the mind becomes obliterated, which creates severe psychological distress. Given the denial to allow one to address the majority of one's basic needs, any form of prolonged solitary confinement can be regarded as torture.

6   Evolution as Evolvement of Needs

Kenrick et al. (2010) suggested that the taxonomy of human needs might be derivable from evolutionary theory. Such ideas provide an entirely new point of view on the evolutionary process. Traditionally, the evolution of species is described as the emergence of differentiating features through adaptation or enhancement of capabilities. Variations in capabilities and features become vast that the general link between various species appears to be lost in the process. The situation may be perceived entirely differently if one approaches the description of the evolutionary process in terms of the development of needs rather than in terms of abilities. From this point of view, with some adaptation, the motivational approach is valid not only for humans but also for mammals, invertebrates, plants, etc. For example, a human's need for water is not that different from that of plants. Moreover, it could be argued that the phenomenon of needs is also applicable to the domain of inanimate matter. The assessment of needs within the evolutionary process provides a common denominator that allows analyzing commonalities between different forms of life as well as domains of nature.

Earlier, we showed that human needs (Kopsov, 2019b) play fundamental roles within the behavioral process and can be characterized as the "engines" which trigger our activities. Human needs also provide criteria for defining the success of our actions. An action is proven successful if it satisfies a need. However, needs continuously adjust to enable adaptation to changes in life circumstances. It is important to realize that needs are not a unique attribute of animals and humans. As already mentioned, from the behavioral perspective, humans' need for water is not different from that of a plant. The assessment of needs within the evolutionary process can offer a common basis for describing various life forms that may appear completely unrelated. Accordingly, we propose a model of an evolutionary tree of needs, illustrating the evolvement of needs, as shown in Figure 3.

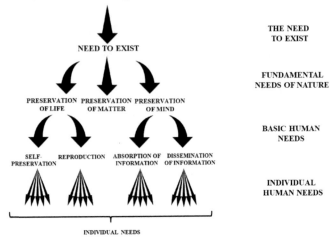

Figure 3. The evolutionary tree of needs.

We conceptualize that the needs of all existing objects and organisms can be attributed to a supreme "need to exist." The origin of the all-empowering "need to exist" is unknown and represents the most profound mystery of the universe. Its resolution, in essence, would answer the question about the meaning of life. The need to exist gives rise to the fundamental needs of nature – needs for the preservation of matter, life, and mind. In the case of humans, the fundamental needs evolve into the basic needs of the body and the mind, i.e., self-preservation, reproduction, absorption of information, and dissemination of information. Ultimately, the four basic needs translate into an assortment of individual needs, desires, and wishes.

Part Four

Human Life as a Course of Evolvement of Needs

7   Human Life as a Sequence of Age Crises

We conceptualize that models and theories of human needs can be applied in the analysis of evolutionary phenomena, including phylogenies, anthropogenesis, or human ontogenesis. This hypothesis is noteworthy, considering that Maslow (1943b) pointed to "the etiology of the basic needs and their possible derivation in early childhood" (p. 395) as one of the key problems requiring further analysis.

Many theories attempt to define stages of personal development, with some gaining significant recognition. Often, they tend to concentrate on childhood, as there is a particular demand for such knowledge from parents and educational institutions tasked with children's upbringing and schooling. We see a prevailing interest in childhood and lesser attention to adulthood as a weak point of conventional theories of personal development. Moreover, most of the underlying research is mainly observational. As a result, scholars failed to provide objective criteria for the periodization of life and identify the causes for alterations in life stages. The primary challenge is that human development is governed by many factors of different origins, such as physical abilities, sexuality, cognitive development, and social skills. Levinson remarked that:

> The study of the life course has presented almost insuperable problems to the human sciences as they are now constituted. Each discipline has claimed as its special domain one aspect of life, such as personality, social role, or biological functioning, and has neglected the others. ... The resulting

fragmentation is so great that no discipline or viewpoint conveys the sense of an individual life and its temporal course. (Levinson, 1986, p. 4)

Levinson theorized that life course is formed by alternating a series of life structure building and transitional periods. The primary task of the life structure building period is the enhancement of life while striving for balance and stability. Subsequently, life structure gets superseded by a transitional period which terminates the established life order and prepares the grounds for a new one:

The primary tasks of every transitional period are to reappraise the existing way of living, to explore possibilities for change in the self and the world, and to move toward commitment to the crucial choices that form the basis for a new life order in the ensuing period. Transitional periods ordinarily last about five years. Almost half our adult lives is spent in developmental transitions. (Levinson, 1986, p. 7)

When the transition period ends, it paves the way to a new life order, which will eventually get challenged too.

We embrace the notion of multiple transition periods and posit that they are triggered by age crises. Further, we hypothesize that age crises are caused by a rise of new, previously unfamiliar dominant needs emerging in a specific pattern throughout one's life course. This conceptualization provides a clear, unambiguous criterion for the classification of stages of psychological development. Depending on a life stage, psychological age crises may last from several weeks in infancy to several years during adulthood until an individual acquires a new set of skills allowing them to deal with newly emerged needs, which can be of different origins. By integrating theories of human development and human needs, we resolve the issue of fragmentation of doctrines of stages of life. In the given context, concepts of needs of different origins do not oppose but complement each other, thus, allowing for their integration.

Since Levinson concentrates on the periodization of adulthood, it became necessary to include in our evaluation concepts covering childhood, among which Erikson's theory of psychosocial stages (1998) is the most widely recognized. By using these two theories as the basis, we propose an original classification of life stages, age crises, and causing them needs (Table 1 and Figure 5) founded on the following vital postulates:

- Commencement of each life stage is caused by an age crisis,
- Each age crisis is caused by the emergence of a new, unfamiliar dominant need,
- New dominant needs emerge through the life course in a specific pattern,
- Dominant needs causing an age crisis can be of different origins.

After we listed life age crises, it became apparent that they have a cyclic order. This periodicity, while being reminiscent of Levinson's concept of life eras (1986), in substance differs from it considerably, both regarding the number of cycles (eras) and their arrangement. We identify four life cycles, each governed by the evolvement of a specific dominant need: bodily autonomy (Infancy), social autonomy

(Childhood), moral autonomy (Adulthood), and physical and social demise (Old age). A motto captures the central theme of each life cycle. For infancy, it is "I want to control my body!" The motto of childhood – "I want to fit in!". For the life cycle of adulthood, it is "I want to be myself!" and for Old age – "I do not want to die!"

A sequence of age crises defines each life cycle. At least three crises always appear in each cycle (relating to different dominant needs): self-affirmation, self-empowerment, and autonomy crises. These crises mark the beginning, the peak, and the end of a life cycle. For example, the four life cycles start with the following self-affirmation crises: the establishment of the biological self (birth), the establishment of the social self, the establishment of the moral self, and the commencement of demise.

Similarly, life cycles end with autonomy crises, i.e., attainment of biological autonomy, attainment of social autonomy, attainment of moral autonomy, and the end of demise (death). Throughout a life cycle, the three recurring types of age crises may overlap with other supplementary age crises. The most acute age crises occur when several new dominant needs arise simultaneously. A typical example of such an acute crisis is birth when multiple physiological needs kick off concurrently in addition to a need for an adaptation to a social environment. Similarly, an adolescent crisis is caused by a combination of the evolvement of sexual needs and a need for social independence. Adolescence crisis also illustrates a case when an age crisis is caused not only by needs dominant in a particular life cycle (social needs in case of childhood) but other kinds of needs as well (biological need of sexual desire). Sometimes a dominant need can have a multifaceted arrangement, resulting in a series of corresponding age crises. For instance, a need for bodily empowerment during infancy manifests itself by a sequence of crises related to mastering various bodily functions, such as understanding visual and sensory signals, controlling muscular movements, etc. (Figure 4).

The first age crisis in the course of life is birth, and the last is death. A significant share of crises happens during infancy when primary muscular, sensory, and social skills are acquired (Figure 4). An individual goes through the following crises after infancy: terrible twos crisis (2 years), social empowerment crisis (6 years), two concurrent adolescence crises (11 years) caused by separate needs for sexual self-affirmation and social autonomy, early adulthood crisis (19 years), age of Christ crisis (33 years), middle age crisis (40 years), early old age crisis (65 years), senility/disability crisis (65+ years), and death. It is noteworthy that all references to the specific age spans of life stages and age crises are tentative. The pace of physical, psychological, and social development varies between civilizations and changes throughout the evolution of humankind. For example, in the not-so-remote past, persons in their mid-teens were mature individuals, while the latest studies lift the endpoint of modern-day adolescence to 24 years (Orben et al., 2020; Sawyer et al., 2018). Within our classification of life stages, reference to particular ages is secondary, as it is not the age per se that defines stages of life, but the occurrence of life crises, the specific timing of which may depend on a variety of individual and social factors.

Table 1. Need-based categorization of age crises, life stages, and life cycles.

No	Life cycle	Age tentative	Crisis	Crisis triggering need
1	Infancy	0	Birth	Bodily self-affirmation - need to establish the biological self
2		0+	Mid-infancy	Bodily empowerment - need to understand visual signals
3		0+	Mid-infancy	Bodily empowerment - need to understand sensory signals
4		0+	Mid-infancy	Bodily empowerment - need to control muscular movements
5		0+	Mid-infancy	Need to understand simple social signs
6		0+	Mid-infancy	Need to generate simple social signs
7		1-1.5	End of infancy	Bodily autonomy - need to establish bodily autonomy
8	Childhood	2	Terrible twos	Social self-affirmation - need to establish the social self
9		6	Middle childhood	Social empowerment - need to master social interactions
10		11	Adolescence no 1	Social autonomy - need to establish social autonomy
11		11	Adolescence no 2	Sexual self-affirmation - need to accept yourself as a sexual being
12	Adulthood	19	Early adulthood	Moral self-affirmation - need to establish the moral self
13		33	Age of Christ	Moral empowerment - need to contribute to the definition of moral &social norms
14		40	Midlife	Moral autonomy - need to establish your own norms
15	Old age	65	Early old age	Need to accept the deterioration of social status, reduced physiological and cognitive abilities
16		65+	Senility Disability	Need to cope with the loss of vital physiological and cognitive abilities
17		?	Death	Organism disintegration

Figure 4. Infancy age crises and defining needs.

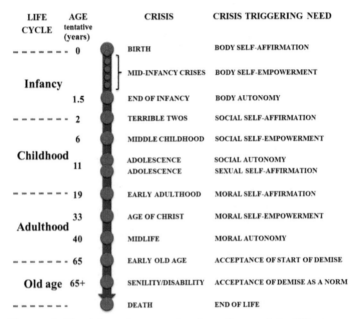

Figure 5. Need-based categorization of age crisis, life stages, and life cycles.

Each life stage requires an individual to develop a new set of skills that was hitherto unavailable to them and entails an adaptation period associated with a degree of psychological disbalance. Plausible to envisage that the psychological response to arousal of a new need goes through a standard coping pattern involving detection of a new need, confusion, acute disbalance, search for a solution, and development of novel skills, resolution, and normalization. Upon resolution of an age-related crisis, an individual's psychological profile undergoes modifications and acquires new qualities. A failure to adapt to an age crisis results in psychological and (potentially) social difficulties later in life. People cope with many crises on a personal level, for example, the midlife crisis (although social factors play a role). However, some crises require significant involvement from parents, family, and social institutions. Anticipation of age crises can allow their mitigation and ease the adverse emotional impact on the individual.

8   Infancy Age Crises

Like other life cycles, infancy contains the three recurring age crises of self-affirmation, empowerment, and autonomy. The central theme of the infancy life cycle is obtaining control over our body, which starts with one of the most acute crises of human life – birth (body self-affirmation). The subsequent empowerment of the body has a multifaceted character as an individual goes through a series of crises caused by the emergence of the need to detect visual signals, sensory signals, need to control muscular movements, etc. (Figure 4). Infancy culminates with the attainment of physical mobility crisis, and at the end of this period, persons, to a large extent, master body autonomy. During infancy, some basic social needs also come into effect, i.e., needs to understand and generate social signs. The emergence of initial social needs adds to the complexity of age crises experienced in early life.

A unique feature of infancy age crises is that they do not leave a memory trace, a well-known phenomenon called childhood amnesia (Robinson-Riegler B & Robinson-Riegler G, 2012). Typically, first memories begin at two to four years old. Neuroscientists posit that this is due to the insufficiently developed hippocampus, which is responsible for long-term memories. However, there are other intriguing perspectives on this peculiarity of human development.

It is plausible that we do not remember our earliest years because there is no requirement to have such memories, as they have no practical value. Indeed, how would one apply later in life such memories as being breastfed, carried around in a complete state of helplessness, or having no control over defecation? Moreover, such memories, apart from being useless, can be confusing and even destructive if remembered later in old age. It is not coincidental that when the first memories appear around the age of two, humans shift from predominantly physiological development to developing social competencies, which in many instances remain highly relevant throughout one's life.

Another pertinent observation is that infancy memories could harm our psyche and negatively affect our self-confidence. For example, many people are anxious about the experiences formed during their adolescence life crisis, alluding to how painful some associated memories could be. We believe that awkward memories of our teenage years could be proven pale compared to the magnitude of psychological distress experienced in one's initial years. From psychological well-being perspective, infant years may be so traumatic that humans do not remember them for their good. Consider the following life-changing events subjecting human beings to an extreme level of strain - being given birth to, obtaining the ability to distinguish objects and tastes, attaining control over one's body, gaining mobility, and learning comprehension of social communication signals. To appreciate the scale of such enormous transformations, it is important to envisage how some of these events would impact one's current life had one needed to go through them at this point. One can imagine the distress of losing some of these abilities or, conversely, picture acquiring some supernatural skills, for example, attaining the ability to read others' thoughts. Such new capabilities would dramatically upset one's psyche, though, by themselves, they would not necessarily be too dissimilar to the experiences of an infant acquiring recognition of speech.

9 Childhood Age Crises

Unlike Erikson, we do not separate childhood and adolescence but rather see them as parts of a single consolidated life cycle devoted to social integration and shaped by the following age crises: terrible twos, middle childhood, adolescence crisis No.1, and adolescence crisis No.2. The terrible twos crisis is caused by the need for social self-affirmation, which is a period when an individual begins to recognize themselves as a social being and discovers ways of coping with the implications of this. The middle childhood crisis is caused by the need for social empowerment, which requires one to learn how to master social rules and norms.

The childhood cycle of psychological development has a rather complex structure in that, along with the governing need for social integration, it also incorporates new needs of physiological nature, in particular, a need for sexual self-affirmation. These processes superimpose on each other and culminate in the adolescence age crisis, representing not one but two interlinked concurrent crises, one caused by a need for social autonomy and another by a need for sexual self-affirmation. Due to this complexity, conventional theories of psychological development separate childhood (2-11 years) and adolescence (11-19 years) into two different stages of life. Conversely, we argue that separately, they do not qualify to be self-contained life cycles. Only taken together, they form a coherent cycle covering all critical steps of social maturing, from self-affirmation through social empowerment to social autonomy.

10   Adulthood Age Crises

Psychological development during adulthood has received less scholarly attention than that of infancy and childhood. At this stage, various state and social institutions surrender their responsibility for personality development and psychological well-being. Individuals are fully developed and are largely to their own devices. Not surprisingly, psychological research for adults prioritizes the treatment of disorders rather than the guidance of living. Levinson (1986) identifies the following transitional periods in what he calls an era of early adulthood: 17-22 years, 28-33 years, and 40-45 years, which matches our concept of three recurring age crises in each life cycle. We hypothesize that the central theme of adulthood is moral development in the context of the prevailing social norms and doctrines. The age crises of adulthood are caused by the sequential rise of the needs for moral self-affirmation (comply with moral &social norms), moral empowerment (contribute to the definition of moral &social norms), and moral autonomy (define own moral norms). The first and the last crises have established designations, i.e., early adulthood and midlife crises. The crisis of 28-33 years does not have a recognized name. Thus, we find it metaphorically appropriate to call the moral empowerment crisis – the age of Christ crisis. This term alludes to the idea that the turmoil of this period of life relates to an individual's desire to influence social doctrines from a position of respected authority. Among the three age crises of adulthood, the midlife crisis gets most of the attention in academia and from the general public.

For the duration of most of their lives, humans typically strive to comply with the requirements and ideals imposed on them by others and society. During infancy, we do not have autonomy over our bodies, and other beings can direct us around at their discretion. Then we go to school and universities to learn the rules that others have devised. Afterward, we form families and embark upon careers in line with society's expectations. We concur with social requirements as we seek safety in compliance, and our needs are often best satisfied through conformity. We may often thrive the more we comply and even challenge ourselves to do our best to comply. However, there comes a time when we become wise enough to start instating our ideals and establishing our own rules. This realization is not a case of rebellious behavior but rather the beginning of a recognition of our might to define or contribute to the definition of what is bad or good, wrong or right. A new need for virtuous self-sufficiency arises, and one begins questioning former ways of living. The solidity of the status quo may start to crumble and becomes an unstable ground that does not allow sufficient space for moral individuality. This shift happens in so-called midlife identity crises encountered by many during their forties and fifties.

The notion of mid-life crises is widely discoursed and studied, although some remain skeptical about it. Paradoxically, taken in historical context, midlife crisis is a relatively new phenomenon because until recently, most people did not reach the age of 40 years. For example, in the UK, the life expectancy between 1550 and 1850s fluctuated between 30 and 40 years. In the beginning of the twentieth century, life expectancy in India and South Korea was as low as 23 years (Roser et al., 2013). By now, the global average life expectancy has doubled and exceeded 70 years. People began routinely to live and experience what is commonly referred to as mid-life only in the twentieth century. That explains, in part, why there is still a degree of uncertainty and ambiguity associated with midlife crises, and the discourse is not over. For the skeptics, we recommend a brilliant book by James Hollis (1993) *The middle passage: From misery to meaning in midlife*, which provides an intriguing insight into the subject.

Interestingly, reaching a mature age is also associated with attaining wisdom, which is perceived to be a positive feature in personal development. This coincidence may indicate that wisdom and midlife crises are somehow related. Indeed, the difference between them could be a matter of proliferation, i.e., a midlife crisis is a mass-produced version of wisdom.

While there were few wise people around, they were revered and listened to. However, because wisdom became a common commodity, it does not get special attention anymore, and individuals are left to their own devices.

Is it possible to avoid the mid-life crisis or at least moderate it? Like other age crises, the mid-life crisis is caused by the rise of a new need, in this instance, a need for moral autonomy, which represents a formidable challenge. It may take several years to develop a new set of skills that allows one to tackle it. The midlife crisis is primarily about advancing one's individuality over group dominance, self-sufficiency over compliance, and moral autonomy over moral conformity. Therefore, perhaps, the mid-life crisis can be mitigated if these character features are fostered early in life.

11   Old Age Crises

All age crises preceding the old age are about enhancing skills (experience) in response to the arousal of new needs. The characteristic feature of the old age crises is a reverse causality between needs and abilities. It is not new needs that require the attainment of new skills, but the demise of skills causing new needs, i.e., needs related to coping with the deterioration of physiological, cognitive, and social functions. The main three old age crises are early old age, senility/disability, and death. Early old age is a crisis of affirmation of the inability to live as a "normal" self. It is triggered by the need to accept and cope with the deterioration of social status and reduced physiological and cognitive abilities. The senility/disability crisis is caused by the loss of vital physiological and cognitive abilities. At this stage, disability becomes a governing factor of existence. Like the multiplicity of infancy age crises, an individual may sustain senility/disability crisis as a sequence of crises associated with deterioration of a specific function (mobility, health, cognition, etc.). Death, or organism disintegration, is the final crisis of the old age and human life.

Part Five

The Second Law of Psychology – The Law of Congregation

12   How are Humans and the Universe Arranged?

The social sciences are largely influenced by anthropocentrism and cognitive biases historically originating from some religious teachings. For example, according to the Christian doctrine, the world was created as a place of domicile for man who was made in the image of God and destined for "dominion" over the living nature (verse 1:26 in the Book of Genesis). The result of these biases is an exaggeration of the uniqueness of humankind's place in nature. Moreover, humans view the surrounding world from a vantage point where bodily, social, and cognitive perspectives are intricately interlinked, both supplementing and contrasting each other. This complicated rationalization of the world may lead to a false interpretation of reality. A typical example is a dominating misconception of the interrelation between mind and culture, which we would like to address.

It is common knowledge that atoms form materials; trees gather in forests; people establish groups, among others. Such is the world in the way we are used to seeing it, and we cannot imagine it in any other way. However, it could have been different – and the universe could have consisted of separate unbonded components, i.e., detached atoms, standalone trees, and isolated individuals. We postulate that a solitary existence is an exception because of the law of congregation, one of the essential laws of the universe, whereby everything seeks congregation and "unity." Components of the universe attempt to evade detachment and instead seek togetherness, as unity assures stability and conserves energy. The universe itself is a congregation of congregations from all domains of nature, with atoms congregating into substances, organisms forming congregations of organisms, and minds congregating into cultures.

These are not trivial observations. The uncluttered understanding of the phenomenon of the congregation concerning different domains of nature allows for challenging some of the conventional paradigms of psychology and the social sciences. For example, we contest a dominant postulate according to which culture/society stands as a separate domain of nature superior to that of minds/humans (e.g., Henriques, 2011). We do not subscribe to this notion and instead hypothesize that culture is not at a level above the mind but amalgamated with it and the two and inseparable from one another. In our previous work (Kopsov, 2021a), we demonstrated that in the generally perceived progression of the evolvement of the levels of complexity of nature matter-life-mind-culture, the latter transition (mind to culture) could not be authenticated. The homogeneity of processes of individual and group behavior leads to the proposition that the human mind/psyche and culture belong to the same level of complexity of nature. This notion challenges the commonly held perception that society/culture is a standalone category of reality supervening the mind.

There are additional arguments supporting this point of view, as it is plausible to reason that the functioning of mind and culture are conjoined, whereby one cannot exist without the other. The mind cannot sustain its existence outside of the social domain, which may appear counterintuitive, as individuals can technically survive outside society. However, this could only ever be feasible for only a single generation. The mind can maintain a short-term isolated existence but will go extinct without social interactions. Hence, it can be concluded that the mind does not exist without society/culture, and society/culture cannot exist without the mind.

The Italian philosopher and novelist Umberto Eco proposed that every cultural phenomenon represents communication (Caesar, 1999). Similarly, Lotman (1990) described the main functions of culture as resisting entropy, storing information, and facilitating communication between people. These views correlate to our notion that the preservation of the human mind, and by extension, human life, is conditional to the satisfaction of needs for absorption and dissemination of information. In this regard, culture provides an environment for satisfying these needs and caters to the most basic conditions of the existence of the human mind.

This argumentation is not constrained to a particular taxonomy of domains of nature. An alternative to the matter-life-mind-culture representation of levels of nature would be the following categorization: subatomic particles, atoms, molecules, cells, organic structures, multi-celled organisms, consciousness, and society. This classification also explicitly distinguishes between consciousness and society. In fact, all known classifications of the primary domains of nature contain a divide between mind and consciousness on one side and culture, society, and civilization on the other. We maintain that such distinctions are incorrect and that mind and culture are wholly integrated. One of them cannot exist independently without the other, and the same principles govern their functionality. Culture does not supervene minds but rather unites them and is a representative of the phenomenon of the congregation of minds.

Matter, life, and mind follow different behavioral principles. Matter can and does exist without life (biological organisms), and life can exist without the mind. Therefore, matter, life, and mind are separate domains of nature, while culture is not.

Furthermore, we consider that society is not a unique attribute of Animalia or humanity, but rather a general framework for the existence of all forms of nature. In this way, a material substance represents a community of atoms. In the biological domain, individual living organisms establish their communities, i.e., the congregations of organisms. Similarly, individual minds form cultures when aggregated. In the cosmogenic context, the social phenomenon evolves through a progression from material substance to a community of organisms and then to cultural formations. In general, the arrangement of the universe is governed by the law of congregation, according to which all basic components of nature, i.e., atoms, organisms, and individual minds, do not exist autonomously but establish congregations, i.e., substances, congregations of organisms, and cultures.

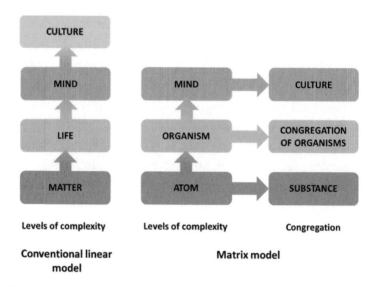

Figure 6. The evolvement of levels of complexity and congregations. Conventional linear and revised matrix models.

This approach (Figure 6) represents domains of nature not as a conventional linear progression of matter-life-mind-culture but as a two-dimensional matrix of individual elements (atom-organism- mind) and their aggregations (substances-communities of organism-culture). Humankind is a combination of two social phenomena: a congregation of organisms and a congregation of minds.

The law of congregation requires a rethinking of the general consensus on evolution. This includes the Darwinist concept of human evolution, which is one-sided and focuses on the evolvement of individual organisms. The evolution of animals, including humans, comprises the evolution of both individual organisms and the societies they form. Consequently, the survival of congregations is one of the driving forces of evolution. Modern science tends to overlook this factor. According to traditional views, human evolution is stagnant due to the minuscule rate of recorded DNA changes.

In contrast, we believe humanity is undergoing a period of rapid evolution. However, it is primarily driven by societal evolution, not by evolution in the Dawinstic sense. Alterations about to happen to humans will be tangible and substantial equal or exceeding the consequences of a major reformatting of human DNA.

We believe that the role of psychology in the analyses of social processes is grossly undervalued. From the vantage point of the universality of the congregation phenomenon, examining society separately from the human mind and psyche equates to studying material substances while ignoring their atomic composition. Even though such an approach may still be plausible and even carry some benefits, disregarding atomic properties in the analysis of materials would remain a grave error given the current state of knowledge. Analogously, social sciences, such as sociology or political studies, must integrate analyses of the human psyche to become a truly comprehensive research field. The continued concealment of the interconnections between the mind and society prevents unraveling the psychological drivers of social phenomena.

The apparent divide between psychology, on the one hand, and sociology and political sciences, on the other, is not well reasoned. We consider that events of political and social natures primarily originate within the domain of human psychology. Human psychology does not only contribute but defines such fundamental and complex social phenomena as ethical doctrines, generational conflicts, civilizational confrontations, and social revolutions. From this point of view, moral and ethical confrontations determine which mental pictures are accepted and furthered by social groups in the overall process of preservation of the mind. We are confident that further study into the competition for cognitive informational domination and cognitive informational collaboration will spearhead new knowledge on psychological drivers behind social processes, both from current and historical perspectives.

Individuals have a dual nature comprising body and mind. Similarly, society is a form of existence of human bodies and minds. It plays a dual role by organizing the lives of organisms and integrating minds. Provision for the continued existence of biological organisms and the functioning of minds are primary; yet segregated undertakings of every social group. Furthermore, as the body and the mind exist through collaboration and mutual antagonism, groups exhibit similar complementary and confrontational aspects related to these two sides of human nature. Groups also generate tensions between individuals, as well as between society and individuals. However, interactions are not necessarily hostile or competitive. Depending on existing circumstances, individuals may choose to support one another. Similarly, individuals and society may foster mutual prosperity. In that regard, moral notions, for instance, altruism or dispensing care for another, are not purely ethical or moral concepts, but demonstrations of the law of preservation in social settings.

Part Six

The Third Law of Psychology – The Universal Process of Behavior

13   How Humans Behave

Behavioral models have been conceptualized within different branches of physiology, psychology, and the social sciences, with varying degrees of concretization. Developed in the early twentieth century, the pioneering theory of animal and human behavior was the S-R (Stimulus-Response) model (Pavlov, 2010; Thorndike, 1898). The model establishes a causal dependency between action and an internal or external stimulus, whilst the organism itself is considered to remain passive and its response predetermined. To account for the individual's active role, the S-R formula was extended to the S-O-R, Stimulus-Organism-Response, conceptualization (Woodworth, 1918), in which the organism plays an essential role in defining its response. Further analytical elaboration of the "organism" component proved challenging for psychology scholars. However, this approach flourished in practical applications, such as management theories, warfare, and decision-making. Several enhanced models were proposed, including the S-O-B-A (Stimulus-Organism- Behavior-Accomplishment) and S-O-B-C (Situation-Organism-Behavior-Consequences) models (Luthans & Davis, 1979). Galperin (1976) developed an M-C-P-CA concept (Model-Clarify-Plan-Control Action), while military strategist Boyd (2018/1987) formulated an O-O-D-A loop defining a decision cycle as consisting four primary steps: Observe-Orient-Decide-Act. Within psychological research, the development of a model of human behavior has largely stagnated.

We consider the enhancement of the model of human behavior as a precondition for the long overdue transformation of psychological studies into the rank of a "proper science."

Further, we describe an analytical model of human behavior, defining a behavioral act as a sequence of the following steps: signal(s)-Detection(D)-Appraisal(A)-Intent(I)-Risk analysis(R)-Act(A). Figure 7 (Kopsov, 2021a) illustrates it in the form of a process diagram. We call this model sDAIRA, which is an abbreviation formed by the first letters of sequential behavioral steps, and which also happens to resemble a girl's name of Spanish and Greek origin, Daira, which means "knowing, informed, wise." While reflecting the complexity and uniqueness of human behavior, the model:

- Defines a process diagram of the behavioral act,
- Identifies four types of components of the behavioral process: main behavioral act steps, regulating blocks, feedback loops, and transfer functions,
- Replaces the Stimulus-Response formula with the Signal-Response principle,
- Reveals the uncertainty of outcomes of a behavioral act,
- Considers both present activities as well as future-orientated goals and aspirations,
- Links human behavior to the basic principles of the functioning of physical matter and biological organisms.

Further, we describe the main features and reasoning behind the new model of a behavioral act. Humans are immersed in a vast array of stimuli originating from physical, physiological, psychological, and social signals. Before further processing, signals must be detected (this is the first phase of the behavioral cycle). However, not all signals are detected;

many are missed or not recognized due to the limitations of the sensory system.

Upon detection, a signal must be assessed with regard to its significance to human existence because not all signals are relevant in the context of life. For example, oxygen availability has no significance under "normal" life circumstances, despite being one of the critical preconditions to an individual's survival. The fact that an assessment occurs implies that a comparison against a set of "criteria" must take place. We refer to such "criteria" as human *needs*. In the long-term, needs may establish stable patterns, but in momentary perspectives, they form a highly volatile accumulation of distinct needs, wants, and desires – all of which are highly affected by extrinsic (outside environment) and intrinsic circumstances (internal physiological and psychological states).

If an individual ascertains a signal relevant to satisfying a specific need, it translates into a stimulus of a behavioral act, and the next step of the behavioral process commences formulating an intent (devise a plan) for action. Planning requires the existence of relevant knowledge and skills that allow one to contemplate a course of action. Hence, the behavioral model includes an *experience & capabilities database*, which represents a repository of all the knowledge and skills of an individual. It contains practical lessons learned and consolidates an individual's attitudes, norms, and cultural predispositions. The experience & capabilities database is continuously updated and altered throughout life.

A devised intent does not imply a commitment to action. It has to undergo assessment from a risk perspective, as individual rates the likelihood of potential gains or losses of action against the criticality of a given need. If a goal can be achieved in different ways, multiple iterations between the risk analysis and planning stages may be required before the individual determines a forward path. If the potential gains are substantial, possible failures manageable, and the estimated energy expenditure acceptable, the individual proceeds to action execution (based on the predetermined plan). On the other hand, if risk criteria are not met, a potential action is abandoned.

The described sDAIRA model of human behavior (Figure 7) identifies the following main phases of the behavioral act: signal(s)-Detection(D)-Appraisal(A)-Intent(I)-Risk analysis(R)-Act(A). *Needs* and the *experience & capabilities database* are not separate steps of the behavioral cycle; nevertheless, they play a pivotal role. Essentially, Needs and Experience & capabilities in combination define human character and personality, Therefore, we also define an extended version of the behavioral model as s-D-A(N)-I(E)-R-A. This format *needs* (N) and *experience & capabilities* (E) are included in brackets as they are not part of the action sequence but rather provide input at its *assessment* and *intent* stages.

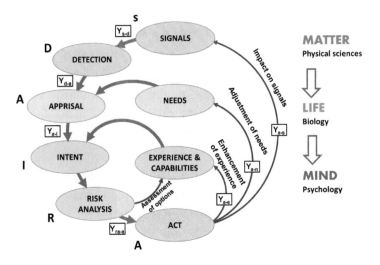

Figure 7. The sDAIRA process diagram of human behavior and phases of its evolvement.

We categorize the components of the behavioral diagram into four primary types: main process steps, regulating blocks (Needs and Experience & Capabilities), feedback loops, and transfer functions (denoted by the **Y** symbol in Figure 7). Transfer functions are necessitated by the fact that each phase of the behavioral sequence operates using unique principles. The exchange of information between phases requires a "translator." The transfer function translates one system's outputs to another's inputs.

According to the model, actions are initiated and then executed based on signals, dominant needs, and the experience & capabilities database. In turn, the outcomes of actions affect future signals, update the experience & capabilities database, and redefine the needs catalog, which triggered the actions in the first place. Consequently, the model includes several feedback loops: (1) intent – risk analysis – experience &

capabilities – intent (IREI); (2) experience & capabilities – action – experience & capabilities (EAE); (3) needs – action – needs (NAN); (4) signal – action – signal (sAs). Feedback loops exemplify the reverse effect of the act on the parameters that triggered or influenced it. Feedback loops continuously generate new updates, which create the dynamism of human cognitive and emotional states. Individuals always exist in a state of unbalance, which requires continuous efforts and adjustments to counter, thus, allowing for the preservation and continuity of human existence. The process diagram of the behavior represents a dialectical model of human actions and incorporates non-linear interactive dynamism between an individual and the environment.

The model allows us to conclude that human behavior in its origin is intrinsically reactive, i.e., humans react to signals. The agency of human behavior originates from the power to select and influence circumstances producing signals. Consider how a meteorite speeds aimlessly through the emptiness of the cosmos in reaction to the forces of gravity or a tree passively awaits rain to satisfy its need for water. Human is similarly reactive to impacts and effects, with one essential distinction being that they have an option not to wait for the rainfall but to go to a water source to satisfy the need. They can anticipate and place themselves in a position or situation where desired signals may occur.

An essential feature of the derived process diagram is its ability to address acts of human behavior as well as to model future-orientated aspirations (Kopsov, 2019a). The latter represents future anticipated so-called *deferred needs*. In the case of deferred needs, the *act* stage of the behavioral sequence is absent, and the forecasted behavioral cycle ends with the *risk analysis.* Hence, human aspirations are defined as the sDAIR sequence model.

Previously, we also examined the processes of functioning of groups of various kinds (e.g., project organizations, military units, sports teams), identified their common parameters, and compared them to the process of individual human behavior (Kopsov, 2021a). We concluded that despite some application-specific differences, the operational process is the same for all groups and similar to the generic process of individual behavior (Figure 7).

14   Do we Behave Like Ants?

The theory of psychology is full of voids. One of them is a gap in the conceptualization of how human needs transform into behavioral acts. The reason for this is twofold. The first one is the ambiguity of contemporary theories of human needs. We have addressed this deficiency by developing an analytical model of the four basic human needs (Figures 2,3) derived from the principal laws of preservation of life and mind.

However, there remains a second challenge as the transformation of needs into acts of behavior is understood only for specific life circumstances. For example, the mechanism of motivation arising from biological demands is clear. It is not difficult to define a logic for behavior aimed at the satisfaction of hunger, protection from adverse weather conditions, escape from violence, etc. However, the origin of human motivation in a social context remains obscure. Motivation is studied by a wide range of disciplines, from nursing to theories of social revolutions. They all provide a behavioral rationale for a specific type of activity, characterized by clear decision-making criteria to be used in given settings. Such analyses often imply that people get clear incentives, penalties, or recommendations concerning a preferable course of action. Such clear-cut situations are exemplified by a graduate deciding on a career choice under parental guidance, a constituent voting while expecting a particular benefit from a political party, or an individual observing an ethical code by following traditional social norms. Specific theories studying different kinds of such motives operate with unique behavioral criteria and remain fragmented.

The aforementioned clean-cut situations are seldom present in life, as decisions are often multiphase and criteria are not obvious. In most instances, behavior, behavioral habits, and predispositions develop in circumstances that can be described as ambiguous, unsolicited, and unprovoked. More often than not, life context implies a selection from multiple possible outcomes with an opulent room for a free choice. Humans encounter situations when alternatives are not evident, and decisions are made without awareness of commitment. Such decisions may depend on an individual's mood and extrinsic circumstances, so one is sometimes unable to explain the rationale for their actions. It is a variety of circumstances, nuances, and choices that created such diverse humankind. In that regard, the question of how social settings translate into acts of individual behavior remains open.

Humans are complex beings, and their behavior is equally complex and difficult to study. Given the current primitive state of psychology, building a comprehensive motivational theory by studying only humans is impossible. Due to the phenomenon's complexity, defining an analytical model of behavior-triggering mechanisms is problematic. The analyzed behavioral system needs to be simplified and stripped of nonessential elements to achieve this. That is where comparative psychology comes into play. Comparative psychology is the scientific study of the behavior and mental processes of non-human animals. According to our views, the fundamental principles of the functionality of humans and animals are similar, as they belong to the same level of complexity of nature. The difference is mainly in the degree of sophistication of behavior and the organization of their societies, i.e., the differences are quantitative, not qualitative. The relative simplicity of the activities of animals is an advantage when studying the basic principles of behavior. Further, we examine the simpler forms of behavior and explore how analyzing social animals' activities can help untangle a blurred picture of socially determined motivation.

Let's consider the behavior of ants as an example. One may say that ants are in many ways similar to humans. They appear to possess high moral standards manifesting through self-sacrifice, commitment to social duties, and care for others. They establish elaborate social protocols and demonstrate physical and mental endurance whilst displaying a clear preference for teamwork. Also, they effectively respond to changes in the environment (often through cooperation), excel at building and maintaining complex structures, and exhibit good communication skills.

This seeming analogy of the attributes of ants in relation to humans describes a specially trained task force. In some instances, since possessing a superior sense of smell can also be added to the aforementioned list of capabilities of ants, humans could be inferior to ants. Charles Darwin (1871), in *The*

Descent of Man, wrote about ants with a high degree of admiration:

> It is certain that there may be extraordinary mental activity with an extremely small absolute mass of nervous matter: thus, the wonderfully diversified instincts, mental powers, and affections of ants are notorious, yet their cerebral ganglia are not so large as the quarter of a small pin's head. Under this point of view, the brain of an ant is one of the most marvelous atoms of matter in the world, perhaps more so than the brain of a man. (p. 59)

Humans, ants, and other social beings have many similarities in how they live, and their behavioral patterns are often indistinguishable. Ants possess another remarkable character feature: they appear to dedicate their full attention to a specific task at any given time, such as gathering food, rearing child ants, housekeeping, and defense, which makes them well suited for analyzing behavioral traits.

In Table 2, the behavioral sequences of an ant foraging for food (e.g., Dorigo, 1992) and a human looking to satisfy a need are laid out side by side. Comparing the two behavioral sequences shows that their compositions are the same.

Table 2. Behavioral processes of humans and ants.

The behavioral sequence of ants foraging for food	The behavioral sequence of humans looking to satisfy a need
Chaotic initial movement.	Seek opportunities for satisfaction of needs.
When a food source is found, the route back to the colony is marked with a pheromone trail.	Upon satisfaction of a specific need, this achievement is marked (visually, verbally, in writing, etc.), and a direct or indirect statement of the accomplishment is made, either describing the trail to the achievement or allowing others to estimate such a trail.
The pheromone trail is followed by others upon encounter.	The trail to need satisfaction is followed by others.
Subsequent individuals reinforce the trail by similarly marking it using pheromones on their path back to the colony if they have food.	Subsequent individuals reinforce the trail to the satisfaction of need by similarly marking it through various means.
Upon exhaustion of the food source, no further trail markings are made by returning ants, and the pheromone scent dissipates.	Upon exhaustion of the source of satisfaction, no further markings are made, and the trail to achievement dissipates.
Chaotic movement resumed.	The continued search for opportunities to satisfy needs is resumed.

The actions of ants following the markers left by other individuals are evident in the behavior of other species, including ruminant mammals, fish, and birds. This type of behavior becomes especially apparent in its deviant forms, for example, when the track followed by animals gets looped. In such a case, animals may begin to move in circles endlessly and seemingly purposelessly for hours, days, or weeks, sometimes dying from exhaustion (Baker, 2023; Weisberger, 2019; White, 2022). In other circumstances, a followed track can lead to entrapment endangering animals' lives-

For humans, the presented sequence of steps is valid for most, if not all, social activities, either moving in traffic, job hunting, selecting clothing, or searching for a partner. This behavior is especially evident in its deviant forms, such as mass hysteria, rioting, formation of cults, worshiping of celebrities, etc.

Comparing the behavior of humans to ants shows that humans and other living beings are not too dissimilar, which could indicate that humans ought to become more modest in judging their role and place in the universe. The human sense of superiority impedes interactions with other living beings and obscures the understanding of the humble place homo sapiens occupy in the broader picture of the world. The pretentious human self-perception is primarily instigated by anthropocentrism and cognitive biases originating from religious doctrines.

15   Success Markers

Ants mark paths to success, such as sources of food, by leaving pheromone trails. Bees do the same by performing ritualistic movements, and birds by singing. Humans do it too, but have at their disposal a wider variety of methods for marking success tracks by symbols, written interactions, verbal means, and visual images. We conceive that trailing the markers of success represents the most generic mechanism behind actions of social nature. This concept allows us to unify the fragmented theories of social motivation.

Firstly, humans define a vision of success. Then they link it to a specific set of markers (signs), which they follow. Most social choices humans make are at least partially based on following success track markers laid out by others. This approach is applied to making such important decisions as selecting religious affiliations, places of residence, education, and lifestyle, as well as for more trivial choices such as fashion, music, consumption patterns, and entertainment. Indeed, there are industries dedicated to continuously creating success markers, such as fashion, advertisement and PR, event sponsorships, styling, voluntary cosmetic surgery, and luxury goods. Many tangible social patterns and trends act as success markers, including attaining private education, engaging in certain types of sports, and embarking on prestigious careers. Often, the markers of success can be rather superficial, as exemplified by branded clothing, fashion accessories, luxurious possessions, and celebrity publicity. Some subcultures generate their style of markers, which can appear obscure to outsiders, for example, particular types of tattoos, social rituals, religious pilgrimages, or celebrations of specific accomplishments.

The process of human social activities works as follows: first, success markers are defined, they are then found in the surrounding environment, a route to their attainment is established, and subsequently, this route is recreated by others. This process applies equally to complex life-defining decisions as well as simple, everyday choices.

The theory of success markers provides a unified concept for a diversity of seemingly unrelated psychological, social, and political phenomena, such as the sudden explosive growth of political and social movements, Stockholm syndrome, or a rapid historical rise or demise of political systems. It also offers insight into some basic principles of public relations, propaganda, and marketing. Mentioned phenomena and applications appear to be unconnected. Each with its own set of theoretical explanations. The chance of merging them seems to be remote. Yet, the proposed theory does precisely that. Further, we describe how the theory of success markers can be utilized for various conditions and applications.

Stockholm syndrome is a condition in which hostages develop a psychological bond with their captors. The term goes to 1973, when four hostages were taken during a bank robbery in Stockholm, Sweden. Upon their release, the hostages defended the captors and would not agree to testify in court against them. This psychological condition can be explained by hostages adopting new virtue norms (success markers) conveyed by their hostage takers, hardcore criminals but formidable personalities. After a few days together, victims took the side of the perpetrators and attempted to justify the violence committed against them. This happened within less than a week in the context of very personal, tense communication between hostages and hostage takers occurring in a confined environment. Effectively normal views denouncing criminal acts were reformatted through this event, and hostages adopted unconventional moral stands under the influence of hostage takers. The hostages' traditional convictions became overpowered by the views and principles of criminals, who generated contrasting markers of success.

Similar dynamics can develop on a much larger scale when entire countries undergo dramatic changes in moral and social norms, transforming societies into oppressive regimes within a matter of years. Likewise, these states may undergo an equally fast reverse transformation back to relative normality. Throughout such turbulences, millions of people start to follow new success markers redefining the fundamental morals and the whole functioning of society. These success markers (behavioral norms) are commonly introduced during turbulent times by a small group of strong leaders commanding fear and obedience or, alternatively, respect and admiration.

In modern times, we all witness how novel views in Western cultures can emerge and begin to dominate the social agenda within a matter of years, e.g., climate change and critical race theory. Sometimes new social trends emerge within a matter of months, as happened with a rise and spread of the concept of gender fluidity. It appears that these modern social trends are fueled by the emergence of new generations and facilitated by social media providing an entirely new technology for creating and distributing success markers.

All cases mentioned above are characterized by the rapid spread of new success markers acquiring vast support and instigating rapid changes in standard behavioral patterns. The explosive expansion of certain success markers emerges within specific historical contexts or life circumstances. Such occurrences have become even more vivid in recent times. The introduction of internet and social networks facilitates the conception and quick dissemination of new success markers.

The theory of success markers can explain a wide variety of psychological and social phenomena because it ultimately originates from the previously outlined laws of psychology. It especially strongly correlates to the law of preservation of the mind and the related concept of basic human needs of absorption and dissemination of information (Figures 2,3).

Success markers, in effect, provide a mechanism linking human behavior to these basic needs.

By now, we have built the case arguing the validity of the concept of success markers for describing behavioral triggers in circumstances characterized by a free choice. We hypothesize that humans live within a matrix of competing success markers. Within this matrix, we select a preferred course of action to follow. Further, we will use the concept of success markers to look into some intriguing aspects of the human psyche.

Success markers can be transmitted in a variety of ways. This can be a written record, an image, or even a scent. What is common for them is that they are primarily generated by humans. In this regard, humans are not creators but also carriers of success markers. In fact, humans in themselves (in their posture, behavior, presentation) constitute the most commanding type of success markers. In this setting, a success marker is evaluated not only on the merit of its utility but on the basis of the impression left by the success marker creator or carrier. This phenomenon explains some well-known practices.

For example, fashion magazines always put a human or a human face on the cover. This is because humans and human faces are the most noticeable, powerful, and efficient representations of success markers. Thus, placing them on a cover increases magazine' sales.

For the same reason, any public speaker is judged not only on the message they deliver but on how it is delivered. This is also an explanation behind a popular (although still debated) concept that in personal communication, only a smaller fraction of all interaction is conveyed by verbal means. Whereas the nonverbal component of communication, such as the tonality of the voice and body language, account for its larger share (Mehrabian, 1981). This is because messages are not only judged on the merit of their content but are assessed as markers of success, the potency of which is directly proportional to the credibility of a person delivering it.

The message is designed to be a success marker. However, in many instances, the credibility of the person delivering the message can be more important than the message's merit. The appeal of any individual most vividly transpires not only through a physical appearance but through the allure of the story behind an individual. A powerful success marker always includes a captivating story behind the message or personality delivering it. Therefore, the most commanding success markers are generated when a human provides a story behind it. Politicians and dealers, who have known about it since the time of dawn, always offer a story for the ideas, goods, or services they promote.

The whole social framework can be viewed as a system of success markers. Some of them are individual, but many of them are shared within social groups. This system of markers defines our subjective social predispositions and allows people to establish groups and communities, be that families, social movements, nations, civilizations, etc. Common success markers define communities.

The derived theory of success markers challenges the deeply embedded common perception that individual predispositions, beliefs, and morals are rigid, stable, and unwavering. In most instances, they are. But is it because of the strong personal predisposition, or is it due to the power of the surrounding social environment? The aforementioned cases of Stockholm syndrome, the rapid spread in modern Western society of new views on gender, and the rapid historical rise and demise of dictatorships show that, in many instances, human convictions are not so rigid and can change dramatically within a short time.

Humans are also aware that they play the role of success markers. This self-awareness affects how individuals construct their image and how they perceive themselves. This phenomenon represents a fascinating subject for future research.

16   Uniformity of Behavior of Matter, Life, and Mind

The world comprises endless diversity of matter and life. It is astonishing that in this ocean of variations, scholars succeeded in orderly classifying atoms, rocks, planets, gasses, bacteria, animals, businesses, nations, social formations, and all other phenomena surrounding us. Many generations have worked diligently to learn about every unique component of the world. This knowledge is so vast that a proper comprehension of the universe by any single individual is beyond reach.

We would like to offer a very different perspective on the world and affirm that despite its vast diversity, everything in the universe functions according to the same set of principles. Where traditional approaches distinguish endless varieties, we see homogeneity. We substitute diversity of properties with uniformity of processes. From our vantage point, the world is uniform, and all its events occurring are defined by the same set of rules that are equally applicable to the behaviors of atoms, microorganisms, mammals, plants, humans, social groups, etc. Such conceptualization bares multiple correlations to

Whitehead's (1985) "process philosophy," which approaches existence as a sequence of "acts of becoming" rather than "acts of being." The process philosophy views universe components through the lenses of their dynamic reactions to the surrounding environment rather than static amalgamations with unique properties.

At the core of our paradigm lies an understanding that behavior is a universal phenomenon, not a unique feature of animals and humans (Henriques, 2011). In that way, chemical reactions between substances, hibernation of trees, or a lion pack chase of the game, all constitute acts of behavior. The difference between these acts is in their complexity. Accordingly, we have derived (Kopsov, 2020b) models of the functionality of physical objects and living organisms in line with the methodology previously applied to the description of human behavior, as depicted in Figure 7. The outcome was a series of behavioral models for different levels of the complexity of reality, i.e., matter (inanimate matter), life (animate life), and mind (mental phenomena). We conceive that human behavior results from an evolutionary evolvement of behavioral phenomena, which initially concern the "functioning of matter," then develop to the "functioning of organisms," and subsequently extend to the "functioning of minds."

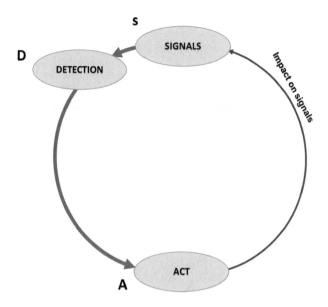

Figure 8. The sDA process diagram of the behavior of inanimate matter.

We propose that the sDA model describes the behavior of inanimate matter, i.e., signal(s)-Detect(D)-Act(A) (Figure 8). According to this model, the functionality of inanimate matter is fully characterized by its properties, which are represented by the detect (D) component of the behavioral model. It stipulates the type and strength of signals that affect the existence of inanimate matter.

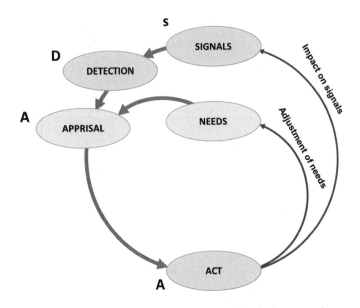

Figure 9. The sDAA process diagram of the behavior of animate life.

The sDAA model defines the behavior of animate life, i.e., signal(s)-Detect(D)-Assess(A)-Act(A), and accounts for the influence of needs (Figure 9). For animate life, such as plants, the detect (D) component is also present; however, the primary element of the behavioral process is the assessment (A) phase, which correlates signals to needs and defines an organism's response to stimuli. Subsequently, human behavior is determined by the sDAIRA model, which incorporates the intent (I) (planning) and risk analysis (R) stages. It represents the most advanced form of a behavioral process, supervening the principles of the functionality of inanimate matter and animate organisms. To illustrate the main phases of the evolvement of the behavioral process (Figure 7), we color-coded its components to link their origin to the formations of matter (red), life (green), and mind (blue).

We stipulate that each level of complexity is associated with a specific dominant element of the behavioral process (Figures 7, 8, 9). For inanimate matter, the governing parameter of the behavioral process is the detect (D) phase which exemplifies the material properties of the substance. For animate life, the critical stage is the assessment (A) of signals against predefined needs. This phase embodies the ability of living organisms to generate an array of complex pre-defined responses to various environmental impacts. Lastly, the behavior of the mind is dominated by the intent (I) and risk analysis (R) phases, which epitomize mental phenomena.

Why do we sometimes feel connected to other forms of life or inanimate objects? The apparent answer could be because they surround us; they define our habitats, and we get accustomed to them. But there is also another kind of connection. The world-famous painter of the "Scream," Edvard Munch (1930-1935), wrote in his notes that "the hard mass of the stone is also alive." This observation is not a theoretical postulation but a personal reflection of an artist deeply immersed in his emotions and the texture of the universe itself. Indeed, rocks, plants, animals, and humans are all elements of the universal evolvement process. They all exist following the same laws, and function following the same rules of behavior. However, the difference lies in the complexity of their arrangements, and the difference is not necessarily as vast as it may initially appear. Some scientists and philosophers also subscribe to ideas similar to those of Munch. Renowned mathematician and philosopher, Alfred North Whitehead (1985), stipulated that perception is not just a feature of living beings but also an attribute of unconscious matter, and argued that perception is the essence of existence. According to Whitehead, the hard mass of rock can perceive and is therefore alive. Of course, the way rocks feel differs from how humans feel. With this understanding, one imagines how we can be drawn to objects and creatures around us, not only because they are part of our habitats but because, in a way, we are similar to them and collectively form a single universal togetherness.

Proponents of panpsychism claim that even the phenomenon of consciousness is not uniquely attributed to the brain, instead, is a quality inherent to all matter. In this regard, "consciousness" is not equated to self-awareness but rather to the ability to experience emotions such as: pleasure, pain, and visual or auditory perception (Goff, 2019).

We have difficulties communicating with people who speak different languages, and except for some rather primitive techniques, we have also lost the ability for meaningful interaction with animals. The fact that humans experience a conscious disconnectedness with rocks and trees does not mean there are no bonds between us – perhaps, we simply lack the means of communication.

The concept of the interrelation of the main principles of the functioning of matter, life, and mind is not a novel one; many scholars have emphasized the connection between life and mind by pointing out that human "capacities of understanding… are rooted in the structures of our biological embodiment" (Varela et al., 1991, p. 149). Proponents of the free energy principle (e.g., Kirchhoff & Froese, 2017; Bruineberg et al., 2018) argue that life and mind share the same basic organizational properties.

Furthermore, scientists discovered comparability between living organisms and non-living systems. The latest studies identified a substantial similarity between the web of neuronal cells in the human brain and the cosmic network of galaxies. Such resemblance suggests that the self-organization of both systems is likely being shaped by similar principles of network dynamics. This is despite their radically different scales and phenomena at play (Vazza & Feletti, 2020).

A study by Volkov et al. (2009) indicates that certain species of plants possess short-term memory, a feature of intelligence. A new study by Adamatzky (2022) suggests that fungi (mushrooms) may also exhibit signs of intelligence as they apparently can communicate. The generation of electrical impulses enables the signal exchange through long, underground filamentous structures called hyphae – similar to how nerve cells transmit information in humans. Mathematical analysis of the electrical signals fungi seemingly send to one another has identified specific patterns in such communications.

Previously mentioned studies (Adamatzky, 2022; Vazza & Feletti, 2020; Volkov et al., 2009) point to commonalities between living organisms, non-living matter, and consciousness. These studies mark a transformation from theorization to experimental studies of interconnections between nature's different levels of complexity. Possible signs of intelligence in biological organisms may indicate that the conceived sDAA animate life behavioral model is more nuanced. Such a finding would not negate the main conclusions of our theory. Moreover, it may lead to an acceptance of the existence of some rudimentary features of intelligence and active perception in the lower levels of complexity of nature. In such instance, while maintaining the fundamental framework of derived postulates, it would be more appropriate to relate to the "dominant" or "prevailing" behavioral processes rather than unequivocal features of defined behavioral schematics. The cases of rudimentary intelligence in biological organisms may represent transitional forms within the progression of behavior from the functioning of life to the operation of the mind. They can be proof of our theory of evolvement of the behavioral phenomenon, in the same way as transitional fossils (Freeman & Scott, 2004) are proof of Darwin's theory of evolution.

The primary idea of our thesis is that the perspectives of matter, life, and mind are interconnected through the common principles of functionality, which can be described by a generic process differently configured for different levels of complexity. The process diagram of human behavior (Figure 7) illustrates the most multiplex type of behavior. Algorithms corresponding to matter and life represent simpler versions. Comparing the three presented process diagrams (matter, life, and mind) provides a unique perspective on evolution from the physical to the biological and, subsequently, to the psychological dimensions (Figure 10). It allows the identification of common functionality features of physical objects, biological organisms, and animals/humans. All process schematics are fundamentally based on the Signal-Response principle; they begin with a signal and end with action. Signals require filtering and gauging; therefore, signal detection is a common and integral part of all systems. All schematics include a feedback loop, which identifies a reverse impact of an action on the signal that triggers it. The emergence of other components of the operational processes can be seen through the lenses of consequential phases.

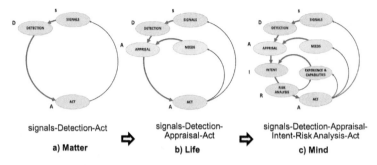

Figure 10. The evolvement of behavioral processes: from Matter to Life, from Life to Mind.

The evolution of behavioral processes occurs through the emergence of new steps and new feedback loops. Throughout this development, functional processes of higher complexity do not invalidate previous principles of behavior but supervene and incorporate them into more advanced forms. The processes of biological nature emerge from the physical matter behavior through the addition of needs and need appraisal modules. In turn, the processes of psychological nature emerge from the biological behavior through the addition of intent, risk assessment, and accumulation of experience. Through this progression, each level of complexity becomes associated with the emergence of specific components of the behavioral process.

Transformations occur through shifts from immediate and predetermined reactions exhibited by physical objects to long-term orientated and variable responses, as in the case of humans. One may say that objects have set characteristics, whilst humans have characters (free-willed personalities), and as objects produce a reaction, humans take action. The underlying theme for all changes is the increasing prominence of the future orientation of behavior. The transient existence of physical objects contains no future awareness; their future perspectives transpire only through the dynamic nature of signal-response interactions. While concentrating on present-time objectives, biological organisms exhibit future orientation through genetic encoding.

Finally, furthest along the evolutionary chain, human lives primarily aim toward achieving future-orientated goals. The rise of the future orientation of actions is a prominent feature in the evolvement of the behavioral phenomenon and one of the driving forces behind it. This hypothesis is particularly plausible in light of the concept of the free energy principle, stipulating that systems maintain their existence by trying to minimize the "surprise" factor, defined as the difference between a system's model of the world and its actual perception of the world (Friston, 2010). The future orientation of behavior aims to minimize surprise; for example, within the process of human behavior (Figure 7), this is realized through analysis of risks, planning, accumulation of experience, and adjustment of needs.

The evolutionary trend toward the future orientation of behavior occurs alongside the enhancement of information processing and storage capabilities. In a familiar pattern, lower-level information processing becomes integrated into more advanced and complex systems (Henriques, 2011). The phenomenon of information emerges in the material matter – as the atomic arrangement by itself represents a record of information. While absorbing inanimate nature properties, biological organisms acquire a more advanced genetic information feature. Animals and humans capitalize on the genetic system and develop the psyche and mind enabled by neuronal information processing. It is plausible to argue that each domain of complexity is enabled through the emergence of specific modules of the behavioral process diagram and associated information processing type.

The "detect" module in the behavioral schematic of physical objects is related to the arrangement of subatomic particles. It represents core material properties and an atomic means of information storage. The emergence of the "appraise" function correlates with the formation of biological organisms and genetic information encoding. Intent and risk assessment modules enable the psyche and mind through neuronal information handling.

Henriques (2003, 2011) postulates that all categories of nature are characterized by shared fundamental phenomena such as information processing and behavior. We elaborate on this by suggesting that the fundamental phenomena also include a governing law of preservation and a congregate class. Hence, for each category of nature, a set of shared essential characteristics includes behavior and an associated governing function of the behavioral process (ref. Figures 7, 8, 9, 10), governing law of preservation, a governing information processing type, and a congregation class, as presented in Table 3.

Table 3. The fundamental characteristics of categories of nature.

	Fundamental characteristics of categories of nature				
Category of nature	Basic component	Governing law	Governing behavioral function	Governing information processing type	Congregation class
Matter	Atom	Conservation of mass & energy	Detection	Anatomic encoding	Substance
Life	Organism	Preservation of organisms	Appraisal	Genetic encoding	Congregation of organisms
Mind	Individual mind	Preservation of cognitive information	Intent and Risk analysis	Neuronal/ Symbolic/Co mputational processing	Culture

It should be précised that the fundamental characteristics presented in Table 3 are governing rather than exclusive. For the matter, the governing function of the behavior is the detection of signals exhibited through material properties; the principal law of existence is the law of conservation of mass and energy; information is preserved through atomic arrangements; material substances exemplify the congregation. For living organisms, behavior is governed by the function of appraisal of signals against predefined needs; the principal law of existence is the law of preservation of organisms; the governing type of information processing is genetic encoding; and communities of organisms represent the congregation. For the mind, behavior is primarily affected by planning and risk analysis activities; the principal law of existence is the law of preservation of cognitive information, which in turn is enabled by neuronal processing; the congregation is represented by culture.

Table 3 summarizes the three governing principles that define the universe as we know it - the laws of preservation, congregation, and behavior. The law of preservation establishes the reason for existence; the law of congregation establishes the form of existence, and the law of behavior defines the process of existence. The primary laws address the core metaphysical questions – why we exist, how we are organized, and how we function. These main universal principles subsequently diverge into more specific doctrines defining the existence of matter, life, and mind.

Thus far, identifying common trends in the evolvement of behavioral principles has allowed us to hypothesize the evolutionary flow between the dimensions of reality (i.e., matter, life, and cognitive mind). This process can be ably depicted by an evolutionary step ladder (Figure 11), describing the accumulation of complexity in behavior, information processing, and preservation drivers during the evolution of nature from matter to life and then to mind.

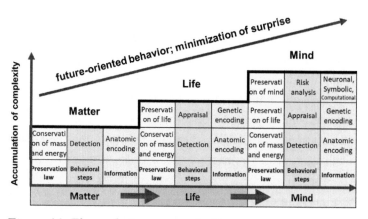

Figure 11. The evolutionary step ladder.

The identified common trends can provide a view on the direction of future evolution. It is most plausible that evolution is an ongoing process and that humankind and nature, in general, continue to evolve (Korotayev, 2018; Kurzweil, 2005). Through forwards extrapolation of defined common traits, we contemplate that the behavioral principles will continue to evolve through the following alterations:

- Addition of new behavioral process steps,
- Addition of new behavioral process feedback loops,
- Increasing future-orientation,
- Addition of a new category to the law of preservation,
- Addition of new information processing methods, and
- The emergence of new types of congregations.

These evolutionary developments will most likely instigate the emergence of new levels of complexity of nature in the future.

The defined trends of the development of behavioral phenomena can also be applied retrospectively. The most basic among the discussed cases is the algorithm of the functioning of physical bodies. However, even that algorithm is characterized by a degree of complexity, i.e., signal detection and information recording through the atomic arrangement. Such features reflect variations in material substances and their properties. It may be argued that an even more basic version of the algorithm exists, representing a state with limited or no variation in a material's nature, indicating an entirely homogeneous state of matter within a highly unified field of stimuli. Such matter may function according to the genuine Signal-Response algorithm containing only "signal" and "action" steps.

17   What Is It Like to Be a Bat

In his since-renowned paper *"What Is It Like to Be a Bat?"* philosopher Thomas Nagel (1974) argues that because bats uniquely rely on echolocation to absorb information, the true understanding of a bat's consciousness is incomprehensible to anyone who's not a bat. One can imagine how it would be like if one were a bat, but not how it is for a bat to be a bat. Therefore, Nagel reasons that in the broader context, every subjective experience is connected with a "single point of view." As a result, it is unfeasible to consider any conscious experience as "objective," which means each individual only knows what it is like to be themselves (and no one else).

However, Nagel did not have a model of human and nonhuman animal behavior at his disposal. He mistook a secondary attribute, i.e., an echolocation signal triggering a behavioral act, as a governing parameter of the behavioral process. Subsequently, he created doctrines of body and mind, subjectivity, and consciousness around a flawed argument. Bats can indeed fly; they mostly live nocturnally, use echolocation for navigation, and have a range of other features that differentiate them from other animals, but these are all secondary attributes of behavior. The primary components of a bat's behavioral process (signal detection, signal appraisal against predefined needs, intent, and risk assessment of actions) are the same as for humans. Bats and humans share more than 95% of their noncoding RNA genes (Jebb et al., 2020), and they share the same principles of behavior. Thus, the question "what is it like to be a bat?" has a straightforward answer - being a bat is not too different from being a human. We have similar worries and daily chores, such as getting food, the desire to procreate, and concerns about our health, well-being, and social status. Even the argument about the uniqueness of bats' navigation using echolocation is now obsolete since recent research proved that humans could learn how to do so (Kolarik et al., 2014).

Dr. Nagel was unable to see the forest for the trees. He and a majority of other scholars are overwhelmed by the variety of elements, components, and species forming the world that they do not come to think that this great diversity is based on a single set of common principles of behavior that keep the world intertwined. Variety in how the world "appears" deceives scientists from uncovering the coherence and unity of the underlying laws of the universe. We argue that the fundamentals of humans' and bats' behavior are the same.

The somewhat amusing question about what bat experiences is closely intertwined with one of the most profound questions posed in philosophy and psychology: "are there knowable universal truths about the world in general and people in particular, or must truth always be relative to an individual or group perspective?" We consider the answer to this question unequivocal "yes- there are knowable universal truths." This is not because humankind possesses superior knowledge (it does not) nor because it is incapable of producing erroneous perceptions (on the contrary, misconceptions have always been an attribute of human mentality). Our postulate is that the human mind is part of the universe and cannot conceive anything outside the premise of the universe. The mind operates according to generic functioning principles and is incapable of producing knowledge disconnected from reality; it is not sworn to truth but part of it.

A single set of behavioral steps defines the behavior of all elements of the universe, though not all steps are evident in some of the "simpler" cases. This set of comprehensive rules of behavior ensures the unity and continuation of the world known to us. It provides us with the means and methods for comprehending reality and allows us to understand the behavior of substances, organisms, and other humans. We possess an inborn notion about how things work because of it. If there were multiple functionality mechanisms, we would likely be unable to comprehend the world fully and only understand those parts of it that function according to our behavior order. However, we cannot exclude the fact that we are surrounded by phenomena we are unable to perceive because they function in ways that are not transparent to us.

Part Seven

Body, Mind, and Society

18   Humans: embodied minds or mindful bodies?

Located outside the city of Naples in Italy, the island of Ischia is renowned for its sand beaches and thermal springs. These days, it is a thriving community and a popular tourist destination. However, there were times when most of its population sought protection within the walls of the Aragonese castle located on a small islet nearby. The fortress's history spanning over millennia accumulated many events, evidence of which can be found within the relics of ancient fortifications, dwellings, and places of warship.

Perhaps, the most peculiar of them is a cemetery of nuns who lived in the castle from the end of the sixteenth century to the beginning of the nineteenth century (Castello Aragonese, n.d.). The nuns were primarily the first-born daughters of noble families, destined for the cloistered life from a young age to allow the family inheritance to go to the first male child. The cemetery consists a series of low vaulted chambers containing the high-backed stone chairs on which lifeless bodies sat. While the flesh was slowly decomposing, the fluids were collected in special jars placed underneath an opening at the bottom of chairs. In the end, the dried skeletons were piled up in the ossuary. Nuns used this macabre practice to highlight the uselessness of the body as a simple container of the spirit. They would spend hours inside the vaults meditating on death and inhaling the fumes of decaying flesh, disregarding their own bodily well-being, fully dedicating themselves to spiritual existence. This practice is a dazing example of how metaphysical matters concerning the relationship between mind and body can manifest themselves in real life. Admittingly, unlike in the case of Castello Aragonese nuns, the issue of interrelation between body and spirit plays a minor role in the lives of regular people.

In everyday living, humans perceive themselves as a solo "I." Within the practical context of living, this is entirely rational. However, this obscures humans' deeply embedded dual nature, consisting body and mind. Their apparent symbiosis covers an ever-expanding rift of different priorities and evolutionary courses, as the body's functioning is governed by self-preservation and reproduction, while the functioning of the mind is governed by principles of acquisition and dissemination of cognitive information.

The mind emerged from the evolutionary development of the body for the purpose of enhancement of organism preservation. However, eventually, the mind becomes so distinguishable that it can be viewed almost as "extrinsic" to the body itself. When we think or conduct an internal dialogue, we address our conscious, our "I-mind." We cannot "talk" to our body; we only perceive its signals. When we cut ourselves, we do not cut our "I-mind;" it is our body that we wound, i.e., our "I-body." In that way, humans are a duo "We" – a cohabitation of body and mind.

Nevertheless, the mind is rooted within the body, affected by the body, and it also, to a large extent, controls the body's well-being. The interrelations between body and mind are both complementary and adversarial as they have particular dominant needs and pursue different priorities in evolutionary development. The mind regularly acts in a supervening manner to the body, and at times, negates it by advancing its priorities at the expense of bodily preservation and reproduction. This antagonism is typified by behaviors such as suicide, childfree living, and unforced extreme risk-taking, which cater to inclinations of the mind but neglect biological needs for self-preservation or reproduction. Generally, humankind is becoming increasingly mind-orientated as the importance of biological factors of existence diminishes. In contrast, cognitive information exchange and acquisition become dominant drivers of economic, political, and even ethical developments.

In our daily lives, we do not recognize that our "compounded nature," makes us two conjoined functioning elements gathered within the boundaries of our flesh. We do not refer to our "I-mind" and "I-body" by saying things like "I-body" would like to get some sleep" in order to take care of my body, or "I-mind" decided to go to a cinema" in order to entertain my mind. Awareness of our "compounded nature" is neither helpful nor rational. At the current stage of evolutionary development, that would be cumbersome. "I-body" and "I-mind" often engage in the same activities, though not always for the same reason. For example, "I-body" consumes oysters or truffles for nourishment, while "I-mind" might be doing it to comply with a societal trend. But it will likely not always be this way, as humanity may be on the verge of a dramatic evolutionary transformation. At that point, the domination of the mind over the body may become even more profound. We risk misinterpreting potential forthcoming changes if we do not embrace our duality and appreciate how the mind and the body have evolved in distinct and separate ways.

Human communities mirror the dualistic nature of individuals. Similar to humans being "the result" of the combination of body and mind, society is a form of existence of two separate but intrinsically conjoined congregations: the population of bodies and the community of minds. As humankind evolves, the balance between the domains of body and the mind within social settings will continue to change as well. We observe it firsthand as the social discourses and international politics become increasingly dedicated to the concerns of the mind, morals, and rightness rather than matters of the body, nourishment, and safety.

19   The Beginning of the End of the Homo Sapiens Era

The universe has evolved from matter (assemblies of atoms) to life (organisms consisting of cells) and then from life to mind (consciousness). There is no reason to believe that such evolutions will cease to continue with humans, who likely represent an intermediate stage rather than the final point of evolution. Retrospective analysis shows that a characteristic feature of such transformations is the acquisition of increasingly future-orientated behavior. We previously illustrated this progress through the following line of examples: rocks cannot predict their future; plants can react predictively but only to a few future needs; then, humans predominantly center their lives on satisfying future needs.

The evolutionary progress of behavior and forecasting skills from inanimate objects to the human mind has been immense. It is not unreasonable to imagine that our forecasting capabilities will continue to evolve at a pace. Sometime in the future, we may be able to analytically model and precisely predict the future state of the world. As a result, the fundamental principles of behavior, as we know them, may become partially invalidated. Some functional components of human behavior, such as action appraisal, intent, and risk analysis, may lose their purpose and be replaced by an absolute awareness of the future. Knowledge will be paramount, and this may represent the next stage of universal evolution.

The mind is becoming increasingly dominant within one host's uneasy coexistence of the body and the mind. Human life becomes predominantly mind-orientated, while the body gradually adopts the role of a "carrier of the mind." Even in this diminished capacity, the body's capabilities are limited, as exemplified by the demise of cognitive functions due to the deterioration of the organism and its subsequent death. The essential capabilities which the body brings to the mind are reproduction and mobility. Since the mind is an information-based system, its reproduction through biological breeding, and the subsequent upbringing of offspring is inefficient and energy-consuming. Other methods, such as digital reproduction, would be easier, quicker, and more reliable. In principle, the need for mobility can be a reason for the mind to continue its bodily existence. However, finding an alternative for bodily means of mobility appears to be more of an engineering and technological problem than anything else. In theory, nothing would prevent the mind from changing its carrier host and even using multiple mediums or means to cater to the need for mobility. In this scenario, the mind would become detached from the human body and become an independent domain of nature.

Suppose the mind eventually separates from its biological carrier by utilizing different information-processing principles and spreads in the form of "a greater mind" (Bostrom, 2014). In that case, likely, humans would not be able to comprehend this new form of mind, how it works, and its motivations. Such a "greater mind" might already exist but be imperceptible to us. Perhaps, if one is to put one's fantasy fully to use, the "greater mind" has created the world known to us, maybe as an experiment, as a sort of informational "backup," or for reproductive purposes.

20   Matter, Life, Mind and a Concept of Time

Time is not a property of an object but a characteristic of a process; it emerges from the interactions between the components of the universe, created by the causality principle that action must cause a reaction. These interactions cannot be conducted instantly; therefore, a perspective of time emerges. If time could have gone backward, then the reaction must have been the cause of action. Within our world, such reversal is impossible as it would invalidate the causality principle of the universe's functionality.

However, this reasoning does not necessarily prove that time could not flow backward. However, if it could, we would have lived in a completely different reality based on a completely different set of laws, which our minds – in their current form – would be unable to comprehend. We would most likely be unable to exist in such a world, either.

The behavior becomes increasingly future-orientated throughout the evolution from matter to life and from life to mind. As already mentioned, human minds primarily focus on attaining future needs. Employees work with the expectation of receiving not an instant but a future paycheck that is spent not straightaway but later; students go to school to acquire knowledge that may only be helpful years into the future. These are future-orientated activities requiring precise knowledge or estimates about forthcoming events. Humans' perception of the future is becoming exceedingly accurate, and we continue to improve our ability to predict it. These improvements are achieved by developing elaborate information processing and storage capabilities and through the enhancement of the scientific conceptualization of the world.

The progress of the evolution of behavior and corresponding forecasting skills from inanimate objects to human minds has been immense. Similarly, one can envisage that our predictive capabilities will continue to evolve and that, eventually, we will learn how to model the future state of the world. Imagine that at some point, humans could accurately predict the state of the world one second ahead of time. As a result, it would be possible to predict an indefinite amount of time into the future by performing continuous one-second future modeling iterations. All future events would become known; behavior then will be optimized; needs satisfied to the highest possible level, and knowledge will become absolute. Time travel within the domain of the absolute knowledge will become possible. As a result, the causal relations between actions and reactions will change, and the notion of time will alter accordingly. Time, as we currently understand it, may take on an entirely new meaning.

In "A Brief History of Time," Stephen Hawking (1988) suggests that time is not uniform and includes three perspectives:

> There are at least three different arrows of time. First, there is the thermodynamic arrow of time, the direction of time in which disorder or entropy increases. Then, there is the

psychological arrow of time. This is the direction in which we feel time passes, the direction in which we remember the past but not the future. Finally, there is the cosmological arrow of time. This is the direction of time in which the universe is expanding rather than contracting. (p. 151)

Perhaps, the "time travel" scenario we describe will not cause a collapse of our understanding of time per se, but rather segregation of psychological time from the thermodynamic and cosmological perspectives of time.

The notions of the emergence of a "greater mind" and the subsequent transformation of time are genuinely perplexing concepts. The former implies a conversion of matter into an objective consciousness, which in turn allows contemplating an idea of a merger of the two opposing camps of philosophy - materialism and idealism. The notion of the evolvement of time travel as a result of the evolution of behavioral phenomena implies that time is a property or derivative of behavior. This line of thinking echoes Hawking's views (1988) on psychological time or Kant's stance on time as not a determination "that belongs to things in themselves" but an essential feature of the human mind (Guyer & Horstmann, 2019).

21   Meaning of Life

In the not-so-far year 2061, an advanced computer begins to understand life's deep fundamentals, enabling it to answer all questions faced by humanity. Eventually, it encounters the last question of them all concerning how the workings of the second law of thermodynamics, which implies the inevitable demise of the universe, can be reversed. The computer responds to the last question: "Insufficient data for meaningful answer." This is the plot of the science fiction story "The Last Question" by American writer Isaac Asimov. The story spans millennia and concludes with the universe dying and a hint of a new one rising in its place.

The last question is also the first question of them all – "Why do the world and life exist?" or "What is the meaning of life?" French painter, Paul Gauguin, reflected on it using his artistic means when creating a masterpiece called "D'où venons-nous? Que sommes-nous? Où allons-nous?" (Where do we come from? What are we? Where are we going?). These matters have been preoccupying humankind from its dawn, and one can imagine Paleolithic age humans addressing similar issues in their stone carvings. Perhaps, the most renowned expression of the mystery of the universal defiance of apparently inevitable dissipation was offered by Shakespearean Hamlet, who famously proclaimed, "To be, or not to be, that is the question."

Within the context of our new paradigm of psychology, we equate the question "What is the meaning of life?" to the question "What is the origin of the law of preservation?" The law of preservation is the primary law of the universe. It stipulates the existence of the world and its components as opposed to nonexistence and vanishing. All other laws originate from it. For the different domains of nature, the law of preservation manifests itself through the laws of preservation of matter, life, and mind. The origin of the law of preservation is unknown to humankind. If we discover the origin of the law of preservation, we will get the answer to the question of the meaning of life.

From a pragmatic perspective, these philosophically perplexing issues are not necessarily critical for a thriving living. Later, we will make a case that the purpose of life is to be happy, and quite plausibly, an individual does not need to possess an awareness of the meaning of life to have a prosperous life.

Based on current knowledge, it is impossible to objectively conclude regarding the existence of the meaning of life, or quote Isaac Asimov's computer of the future, we have "Insufficient data for meaningful answer." Each individual must draw their own conclusions as there are multiple vantage points on the subject. For instance, people following religious doctrines acquire a sense of meaning in life through their beliefs. Contrarily, many scientists may think in similar veins to the renowned physicist Stephen Hawking (2018), who said that "the universe was spontaneously created out of nothing, according to the laws of science" (p. 16). For proponents of such views, there is no meaning in life, i.e., there is no driving force behind life as it arose merely through a combination of some circumstances.

Other scholars, like the former chair of The Department of Astronomy at Harvard University, Avi Loeb (2021), conceive the possibility that a more advanced civilization created our world. Subsequently, such scholars may or may not subscribe to the notion of the meaning of life based on personal views and interpretations. One interpretation could be that through living, we are serving the intent of such a civilization that possesses particular divine virtues. Another metaphysical view could be that humankind is on a mission to become a similarly advanced civilization, and our lives serve this purpose. On the contrary, some may argue that any higher

117

forces are of no relevance to everyday life, and they leave us to our pointless endeavors.

We would like to believe that there is a meaning to life and that it originates from the universal law of preservation. We think humans are part of a universal togetherness with other animate organisms and inanimate objects, all functioning following a single set of laws of being. Each individual contributes to the evolvement of life and the mind. Our ideas, thoughts, and beliefs do not vanish but rather contribute to the overall development of the collective mind, however infinitesimal this contribution might be. The universe's evolvement continues through the inception of new forms of existence. Our life is our contribution to this process.

Part Eight

A Theory of Human Happiness

22   The Desire for Happiness

The human desire to attain happiness has plausibly existed since the dawn of humanity and verifiably since at least the times of ancient Greece. However, its steadfast pursuit is more vigorous today than ever, as the term itself is becoming foundational in political doctrines and cultures across the world. More and more, happiness itself is perceived as a worthwhile goal because it not only feels good but also has tangible benefits for individuals who experience it as well as for their friends, families, immediate communities, and, consequentially, society at large (Lyubomirsky, 2011).

Diener (2013) estimates that the number of scientific articles on subjective well-being (SWB) has multiplied in recent years, from ca. 130 articles published per annum in 1980 to more than 1,000 published per month more recently. However, even as the number of scientific studies of SWB has grown exceptionally in the last 40 years. The concept of happiness remains elusive. However, there is a trend of moving away from descriptive and parametric analyses to creating models of happiness. Csikszentmihalyi (2002), in his theory of *flow* conceptualized happiness as a balance between encountered challenges and the availability of skills to face them. Sheldon & Lyubomirsky (2007) developed a Hedonic Adaptation Prevention model, which theorizes happiness as a balance between present-oriented (*i.e.*, living in the present) and forward-looking (*i.e.*, creating expectations about the future) living. Dodge *et al.* (2012) define well-being as a balance between resources and challenges. Veenhoven (2009), following in Maslow's (1943a) footsteps, proposes a model of happiness based on the satisfaction of experienced needs.

In our view, these models emphasize some specific components of well-being. We attempt to develop a generic model of happiness by postulating that the concept of happiness should be based on the model of human behavior. As behavior manifests itself through actions, then the level of happiness should reflect the level of success of activities undertaken by an individual. It is important to emphasize that we ascertain actions not through simplified lenses of behaviorism but from a perspective of constantly transforming personality in the ever-changing physical and social contexts. We attempt to propose a formulation of happiness, initially for the transient, and then for the long-term perspectives of human existence. We will identify separable components of happiness associated with different needs and time perspectives. We will examine the main factors affecting happiness and discuss variations in strategies for attaining it.

23   Historical Perspective of Happiness

According to McMahon (2006), in ancient Greece, happiness was perceived as being beyond human influence, controlled by luck and the gods. Similar beliefs about happiness were evident in ancient Chinese literature (Lu, 2001). Contemporary Western culture approaches happiness as something over which people can exercise control, actively pursue, and achieve. Hence, throughout centuries, the view of happiness underwent a significant transformation as notions of it turned from non-agentic to agentic (i.e., as something we do not have agency over to something we can directly influence) (Oishi et al., 2013). McMahon (2006) suggests that this occurred through gradual transformation. In the early fifth century, St. Augustine declared that "the earthly quest for happiness is doomed" (p.102) and that true happiness is "unattainable in our present life" (p. 104). A shift can be noticed in the thirteenth century when Saint Thomas Aquinas argued that "the 'theological virtues' of charity, hope, and faith" can grant partial happiness in this life (p. 131). These views signal a departure from beliefs in ancient Greece, where Aristotle and Plato looked at happiness as a state that can be achieved only by a small number of highly fortunate and talented individuals. In the sixteenth century, Martin Luther went further toward the modern view, arguing that "Christians should be merry...To live life as a justified man was apparently to experience the world as a 'pleasure garden for the soul'" (McMahon 2006, p. 172).

Until recently, the path to happiness was one of torment and grief. Wierzbicka (2004) writes, "Misery and suffering are part and parcel of most lives, whereas happiness is not – or so it has appeared to most people at most times" (p. 34). It was only in the twentieth century was it a widely-held belief that happiness was an attainable goal. A noticeable change occurred in the 1920s when the widespread negative religious and moral connotations of happiness started to change. By the end of the twentieth century, the pioneers of positive psychology proclaimed a victory for the belief in a positive human future (Seligman & Csikszentmihalyi, 2000). Pairing the active noun of pursuit with happiness meant that happiness was brought within an individual's reach and control, in sharp contrast to the ancient Greeks' fragile, external view of happiness (Oishi et al., 2013).

The transformation in the meaning of the word happiness is evident through the changes in the definition in evolving editions of dictionaries (Oishi et al., 2013). The 1850 edition of the Webster Unabridged Dictionary includes a clarification reflecting on a view of happiness in the mid nineteenth century, stating that "perfect happiness, or pleasure unalloyed with pain, is not attainable in this life." The modern 1961 edition of the same dictionary provides several definitions of happiness, i.e., "1) good fortune: good luck; 2) a state of well-being characterized by relative permanence, by dominantly agreeable emotion ranging in value from mere contentment to deep and intense joy in living, and by a natural desire for its continuation". Remarkably, the former definition is marked as "archaic," i.e., out of date. This transformation exemplifies how the layman's definition of happiness dramatically altered within a century. In summary, the pursuit of happiness is a relatively new concept, and the notion that a person can be happy is a modern invention (Wierzbicka, 1999). Only relatively recently did the attitude towards happiness change from a passive, extrinsic to an active, intrinsic form.

24   National Perspective of Happiness

Measured levels of happiness vary across nations and cultures. According to the 2015 World Happiness Report, three-quarters of the differences in happiness levels can be attributed to differences in six parameters (Helliwell, Layard, & Sachs, 2015). These parameters are GDP per capita, healthy years of life expectancy, social support (defined as having someone to count on in troubling times), trust (defined as a perceived absence of corruption in government and business), perceived freedom to make life decisions, and generosity (measured by recent charitable donations, adjusted for income).

Economically, prosperous European and Anglo-Saxon countries dominate the list of the world's happiest nations (Helliwell, Layard, & Sachs, 2017). Nonetheless, many of the less prosperous Latin American states occupy relatively high places in the rankings. The top places of European countries such as, Australia, New Zeeland, and the USA, substantially correlate with the six parameters discussed earlier. However, this is not the case in the examples of Costa Rica, Brazil, or Mexico, where the impact of the six parameters has to be adjusted by a disproportionally sizable "residual" component, accounting for "unidentified" factors which the six specific parameters cannot explain.

Such cases of mismatch between predicted and registered happiness levels provide grounds for hypothesizing the existence of a cultural bias in happiness measurements. Proponents of this hypothesis point to several causes for potential discrepancies in cross-national assessments of happiness: (1) linguistic variations in the meaning attributed to happiness, (2) differences in social desirability and moral appreciation of happiness, (3) diversity in response style to survey questionnaires, and (4) potential non-familiarity with the concept of happiness in some non-Western societies. Veenhoven (2009) investigates these hypothetical causes and concludes that there is little empirical data to support the view that differences in happiness can be attributed to cultural bias. However, in contrast to this conclusion, Wierzbicka (2004) remarks that the English term "happy" is used more liberally than its equivalents in French, Polish, Russian, and other European languages. Wierzbicka (2004) further notes that happiness can still be seen as something rare and elusive, but the specific term "happy" has drifted away from happiness to the extent that it can almost be said to be halfway between happiness and okay in the English language. It appears that any conclusions in the debate on the influence of cultural biases on cross-national differences in happiness have yet to be reached. In later sections of this paper, we introduce the notion of multiple strategies for achieving happiness, which may provide a different perspective on why models of happiness vary between nations and cultures.

25   Humankind is Getting Happier

The word "happy" is sometimes used synonymously with "lucky," which also happens to be the original meaning of the word, reflecting on the at-the-time prevailing perception that happiness was only attainable through sheer luck. As it turns out, the specific pursuit of happiness is a relatively modern concept, which began to receive broader recognition in the 1920s, though appearing even earlier in philosophical works and political doctrines. For a majority of previous human generations, life was less about the pursuit of happiness than the avoidance of hardship. The evidence of this is in the books written (particularly pre-20th century) about human pain and suffering, such as many of the acclaimed novels by Dickens, Dostoyevsky, and Hugo.

One can get an intriguing perspective by examining the transformation of comprehension of happiness from a marketing point of view. The popularization of the idea of the pursuit of happiness coincided with the rise of the epoch of mass consumption, enabled by technological progress that could satisfy the needs of a growing number of people. In a way, propaganda of happiness became an instrument of marketing aimed at maximizing the profits of industrial and financial conglomerates. Some of the most widely applied marketing models used for influencing consumer behavior are PMPHS (Pain, More Pain, Hope, Solution) and AIDA (Attention, Interest, Desire, Action). The former marketing model is based on negative incentivization when an individual is exposed to messages triggering discomfort followed by a promise of hope and a viable solution. In contrast, the AIDA model is mostly positively orientated; it avoids the subject of suffering entirely and channels persuasion along with the mindset of positive psychology.

It is notable how the PMPHS sequence accurately resembles the plot of many of the pre twentieth century classic writings, take Hugo's Les Misérables, for example, not to mention the New Testament and passion of Christ. The PMPHS plot is also evident in traditional fairy tales, such as Cinderella or Beauty and the Beast. The same is true about most of the art before the rise of the impressionist era, which is not surprising, as many paintings were inspired by religious connotations, implying pain and suffering as prerequisites of hope. While the PMPHS-based art and literature are still present in the twentieth and twenty first centuries' cultural landscape, they are no longer dominant. On the contrary, the application of the AIDA model expanded considerably in all fields of cultural and social living, vividly illustrated by the emergence of abstract and pop art. One needs to search hard to find any suggestions of pain and suffering in paintings by Kandinsky or Warhol. These artists thrive on the generation of Attention, Interest, and Desire, rendering referencing pain and other experiences of human living unnecessary.

We are not implying that striving for happiness is a cynical marketing plot masterminded by elite capitalists. Conversely, the point is that the emergence of the pursuit of happiness is part of the overall cultural, economic, religious, technical, and social reformation of society, and in a broader sense, a transformation of humankind at large.

Another essential phenomenon came into play in subjective well-being during the twentieth century, as businesses, families, and society at large began to see the benefits of happiness – happy people generally perform better at activities that require high levels of motivation, autonomy, and intelligence. Put differently – and rather crudely – a despondent enslaved person is of little concern, as the unhappy software programmer, primary school teacher, or surgeon would be unable to deliver the quality of work expected from them.

Such observations may appear counterintuitive and controversial as technological progress brought not only material prosperity. It also resulted in the degradation of family values, the demise of the church, the disintegration of social networks, and the collapse of traditional ways of living (Harari, 2015). People have become more susceptible to loneliness, depression, and social pressures. Often, the fruits brought on by modern civilization have failed to transition into the benefits of psychological satisfaction, and new and severe threats to subjective well-being have continued to emerge. These developments are understandable, as we have already pointed out that satisfaction of needs opens up a space for newly emerged needs, which in turn sets the human psyche back into a state of disbalance.

Nevertheless, the positives outweigh the negatives – the notion of universal suffering is continuously fading from modern literature and philosophy as civilization becomes ever more dependent on personal psychological well-being. For many people worldwide, the current generation is probably the happiest generation to have ever existed. However, this positive trend is fragile, as everything to do with the human psyche and public and individual mental health concerns keep growing.

Human life is becoming ever-less orientated toward the needs of the body and ever-more preoccupied with matters of the mind. Material and bodily needs, which were vividly dominant decades ago, have become less critical. At the same time, most of the skills accumulated by humankind precisely suit the satisfaction of these. In the meantime, within the settings of ongoing social and informational transformations, a toolbox of psychological skills addressing the expanding needs of the mind remains underdeveloped. Often, it makes strenuous efforts to match the challenges of ever-changing life circumstances. Unsurprisingly, the mental issues of subjective well-being are taking center stage while people are trying to adapt to new ways of living.

26   Happiness *vs.* Subjective Well-Being

Wilson proposed an early contemporary definition of happiness in 1967 in the paper "Correlates of avowed happiness." Two years later, Bradburn (1969) published "The structure of psychological well-being," which was later regarded as an essential contribution to the study of well-being. Although Bradburn uses the term *psychological well-being* in the title of his work, he also refers to this term as happiness.

Bradburn links happiness to Aristotle's idea of *Eudaimonia*, commonly translated as well-being (Dodge et al., 2012). Since then, the usage of the term well-being has expanded, and scholars eventually amended it to *subjective well-being* (SWB). Ultimately, the ambiguity of defining *happiness* from historical and cultural perspectives caused social scientists to opt further toward using *subjective well-being* instead of *happiness* (Diener, 1984). However, it appears that ambivalence may be related not to the usage of a specific term but more to the subject it denotes. Thus, Dodge *et al.* (2012), in the paper with an appropriate title, "The challenges of defining wellbeing," point that "the question of how wellbeing should be defined (or spelled) still remains largely unresolved" (p. 222), which according to Forgeard *et al.* (2011) "has given rise to blurred and overly broad definitions of wellbeing" (p. 81).

Helliwell *et al.* (2015), while discussing the application of the term *happiness vs.* SWB, state three main strands of arguments against using *happiness* instead of SWB. Firstly, *happiness* is criticized for being narrow since it is one of many emotions, so it may be confusing to use it to cover the broader range of measures that humans experience. Secondly, it is criticized for its breadth since the appearance of happiness, both as an emotion and as a form of evaluation, may cause confusion. Thirdly, there are concerns that the usage of the term *happiness* invites dismissal for its apparent flakiness – a topic to joke about, or to ignore for not being sufficiently serious. However, official institutions such as the United Nations (UN) General Assembly Resolution (2011), the Bhutanese government's national objective of maximization of Gross National Happiness, and the Ministry of Happiness of the United Arab Emirates government are explicit in their focus on happiness and its development. Helliwell *et al.* (2015) advocate using the term *happiness* as it is arguably more widely understood than the more technical description of subjective well-being.

The preference for using *happiness* as a synonym for SWB is not limited to political and popular texts but is also widely applied in the scientific literature (Lyubomirsky, 2011; Rutledge et al., 2016). In this present study, we use the term *happiness* as a synonym for SWB. The term SWB is mainly utilized in the specialized psychological literature, while happiness prevails in texts designated for the general public. In our early works, we tended to use SWB; however, with time, we opted for happiness as a more appropriate designation of the phenomenon in the context of human living.

27   Definition of Happiness

The definition of the subject is the first step to establishing a conceptual model. Dodge *et al.* (2012) performed a multi-disciplinary review of past efforts to define well-being. They conclude that the question of how to define well-being remains unanswered and that numerous attempts have resulted only in a description of well-being rather than a definition. An example of the descriptive approach can be found in the paper by Diener *et al.* (1999). They theorize that:

> SWB is a broad category of phenomena that includes people's emotional responses, domain satisfactions, and global judgments of life satisfaction. Each of the specific constructs need to be understood in their own right, yet the components often correlate substantially, suggesting the need for the higher order factor.

Thus, we define SWB as a general area of scientific interest rather than a single specific construct. (p. 277)

However, in their later work, Diener et al. (2002) define SWB as a person's cognitive and affective evaluation of their life, and it has become the most widely accepted definition. Notably, it is closely related to the definition of happiness provided by the modern Webster Unabridged Dictionary. It is also reflected in the OECD (2013) "Guidelines for the Measurement of Subjective Well-being," which quotes the following recommendation from the Commission on the Measurement of Economic and Social Progress: "SWB encompasses three different aspects: cognitive evaluations of one's life, positive emotions (joy, pride), and negative emotions (pain, anger, worry)" (p. 10).

Diener *et al.*'s (2002) definition provides a solid foundation for developing a model of SWB by identifying its main components (cognitive and affective), and referring to the evaluation process, which implies the existence of a benchmark for such evaluation. Historically, the science of happiness was predominantly about ways to enhance happiness. At the same time, the question of the criteria of happiness has always remained in the background. For example, Shin and Johnson (1978) describe well-being as a global assessment of a person's quality of life according to his own chosen criteria. The reference to "his own criteria" is too vague to be used for any practical application.

Furthermore, the definition of *life* is in itself controversial, as many interpretations have been proposed depending on the field of science and context. McKay (2014) argues that in regard to the existence of an individual, life is the

131

history of activities that an organism undertakes. Hence, the criteria for evaluation of a person's life should be based on the degree of success of the activities undertaken by an individual. Understanding happiness requires understanding the underlying mechanisms that initiate, control and gratify human behavior. Thus, any model of happiness must center around the analysis of the process of human functioning, which can be studied through the lenses of the process diagram of human behavior (Figure 7).

28   Momentary Happiness

Since activities are instigated for the purpose of their successful completion, one can envisage that happiness correlates with the success of actions. Therefore, we will use the proposed process diagram of human behavior (Figure 7) to establish a model of happiness, starting with the momentary life experiences related to ongoing events.

Tay & Diener (2011) pointed out that individuals evaluate needs independently from each other, as there is "evidence of universality and also substantial independence in the effects of the needs on SWB" (p. 364). They observed that needs tend to "be achieved in a certain order but that the order in which they are achieved does not strongly influence their effects on SWB. Motivational prepotency does not mean that fulfilling needs 'out of order' is necessarily less fulfilling. Thus, humans can derive 'happiness' from simultaneously working on a number of needs regardless of the fulfillment of other needs" (p. 364).Every action results in a change (however minuscule) in the level of happiness. Successfully executed actions (where a positive outcome is achieved) enhance happiness levels, and vice versa, unsuccessful actions harm happiness. We define changes in the instant level of happiness caused by action as a variation in *momentary happiness* ΔH_m. Its magnitude is proportional to the relative weight w_i of the need which triggers the action. In our formula, the value of the relative weight of an individual need has a value between 0 and 1, and the combined sum of relative weights of all needs is 1, *i.e.*:

$$\sum_{i=1}^{m} w_i = 1 \qquad (1)$$

Where:
m - the total number of needs of an individual.

Successful satisfaction of a higher-weighted need results in a greater level of happiness. Not all actions have successful outcomes; some only partially achieve their objectives, and others may adversely impact living conditions. Hence, the change in the level of happiness upon completion of action must be proportional to the achievement ratio k_i. The achievement ratio is 1 if a need is fully satisfied and 0 if the need is not satisfied at all. Furthermore, intermediate success states arise when a need is partially met; for example, a person aspiring for a work promotion receives assurances that it will happen but is subject to achieving specific additional realistic criteria. Depending on the subjective evaluation of these conditions, a person may perceive that the need is partially satisfied in the given moment and allocate it a ratio of achievement k_i, which is less than 1 (*i.e.*, partial fulfillment).

There are also actions producing adverse results. A worst-case scenario is when an action results in the termination of a need, *i.e.*, making it impossible to satisfy it. In this case, the achievement ratio k_i equals -1. For example, imagine failing a university examination which results in expulsion, thus making the need to pass exams and obtain a degree obsolete (or much more difficult to such an extent that it becomes unrealistic). Hence, for any given action, the achievement ratio can be between -1 and 1. As it follows from the definition of happiness, evaluation of each action encompasses affective (emotional) and cognitive components. Therefore, the change in happiness ΔH_m as a result of an action addressing a specific need is a function of the need's relative weight and the ratio of its satisfaction and can be defined as:

$$\Delta H_m = F_{affective}(\Upsilon_i k_i w_i) + F_{cognitive}(\Upsilon_i k_i w_i) \qquad (2)$$

Where:

ΔH_m – the impact of the action on the level of happiness in regard to need i,

$F_{affective}$ - the affective component of impact of an action on the level of happiness,

$F_{cognitive}$ - the cognitive component of impact of an action on the level of happiness,

k_i – achievement ratio ($-1 \leq k \leq 1$),

w_i – the relative importance weight of the need triggering the action ($0 < w < 1$),

Υ_i – forgetting factor ($0 \leq \Upsilon \leq 1$).

Murray (1938) notes that a single action can satisfy more than one need. For instance, victory in a sports competition may, to different degrees, meet safety, self-esteem, and self-actualization needs, among others. Therefore, the overall impact of an action on the level of happiness is the sum of the achievements for all affected needs:

$$\Delta H_m = \sum_{i=1}^{n} (F_{affective}(Y_i k_i w_i) + F_{cognitive}(Y_i k_i w_i)) \quad (3)$$

Where:

ΔH_m – the total impact of an action on the level of happiness considering all affected needs,

$F_{affective}$ - the affective component of impact of an action on the level of happiness,

$F_{cognitive}$ - the cognitive component of impact of an action on the level of happiness,

k_i – achievement ratio ($-1 \leq k \leq 1$),

w_i – the relative weight of need i triggering the action ($0 \leq w \leq 1$),

n – the number of needs affected by the action,

Y_i - forgetting factor ($0 \leq Y \leq 1$).

Actions with similar or identical outcomes do not necessarily produce the same change in the level of happiness ΔH_m, as the relative weight of a need is significantly dependent on life circumstances. For example, a meal consumed after a fasting period is likely to result in a more significant increase in happiness levels compared to the upsurge induced by consumption of that same meal in normal circumstances, as the weighting of the need for nourishment is more significant in the former case. Equation 3 reflects this phenomenon, as the relative weight of the need is not a fixed but a variable parameter. Indeed, our catalog of dominant needs is constantly updated as some needs are satisfied, and others are made obsolete. The ΔH_m parameter provides a snapshot of the happiness level change.

Actions form a fluid and constantly changing field of activities, and the implications of each action are multiform. The discrete nature of actions immediately raises the question of what happens to happiness levels after action fulfillment. Successful completion of an action caused by one need inevitably turns individuals' attention to other, dormant, or previously non-existent needs, and the pursuit of happiness continues (Maslow, 1943a). Furthermore, changes in happiness levels depreciate over time. The depreciation rate varies depending on the nature of the need and life circumstances. A pleasant evening spent in the company of friends can satisfy a need for social belonging for several hours. Being in a romantic relationship may have an impact spanning years.

Nevertheless, even in the latter case, the residual level of the surge in happiness diminishes over time and trends toward its initial base level (Stutzer & Frey 2006). Restoration of initial levels of happiness (base levels) originates in the neural nature of human emotions. Schuyler *et al.* (2012) demonstrated that the restoration of the human brain's neural status after exposure to visual stimuli (pictures, *etc.*) occurs within seconds. Electrical stimulation of the human brain influences psychological behavior for a period ranging from tens of minutes to several days, with a typical impact lasting 1.5 to 2 hours (Bechtereva, 1988). Therefore, it is reasonable to propose that the emotional impact caused by an action dissipates similarly, in line with the concept of automatic emotion regulation proposed by Schuyler *et al.* (2012). To take into account the depreciation of the momentary impact of actions on the overall state of happiness, Equation 3 includes a "forgetting" factor Y_i, which makes more relatively recent actions more influential than relatively older completed actions. This factor is also used in the equation of happiness developed by Rutledge *et al.* (2014). They hypothesize that happiness is a function of an action's "certain rewards," "expected values," and the difference between experienced and predicted rewards. These parameters correlate with the achievement ratio and relative need weight in Equation 3. Rutledge *et al.* (2014) do not consider separable affective and cognitive components of happiness. This approach may be entirely plausible; however, little research has been conducted into the interrelation and balance between affective and cognitive components of *momentary happiness*.

29 Anticipated Happiness

Equation 3 represents a functional dependency, describing a change in momentary happiness resulting from a life event. It deals only with transient experiences, and the extent of its validity is limited. Further, we would reason that the proposed *diagram of human behavior* provides grounds for modeling well-being components associated with long-term perspectives of human existence and allows us to devise a separate happiness formula to address this case.

The human brain and the body can endure relatively extreme conditions that are rarely encountered. In everyday life, the difficulty level of most activities we are involved with is relatively low: humans utilize only a small portion of their physical, mental, and psychological capabilities. However, humans are never wholly idle either; thus, we usually exist in a state of partial engagement. Indeed, "stimulus-independent thought" or "mind wandering" appears to be the brain's default mode of operation.

Killingsworth & Gilbert (2010) conducted a study on the experiences of thousands of individuals as they went about their daily activities and found that, on average, study participants reported their minds wandering 47% of the time. The study suggested that in the mind-wandering state, people reported being less happy than when they were focused on an activity.

We conceptualize that in periods when individuals are not fully engaged in implementing actions, they continue to be perfectly aware of their dominant needs. The critical difference is that many of these needs are *anticipated needs* that may require a future effort but no immediate action. Per Figure 7, the sequence of steps within the standard behavioral process is signal detection, signal assessment, intent, risk analysis, and action implementation. We propose that the series of steps in response to *anticipated needs* must be the same as for instant needs other than for the implementation stage, which is omitted in case of *anticipated needs*. Thus, intent (planning) and risk assessment are the concluding steps of the *behavioral process* for *anticipated needs*. Planning is a linear operation, often performed within a loop of iterations combined with risk analysis. Concerning future actions, planning can only be completed to a limited extent. Unlike planning, risk analysis represents a decision-making gate implying the application of different and, at times, contradicting criteria and requiring allocation of a criticality rating to the input and output parameters in situations of uncertainty. These factors make risk analysis the most complex and crucial stage of the *process of human behavior*.

We postulate that, particularly in the case of *anticipated needs*, happiness is determined not by the outcome of the action itself but by the result of the risk assessment of the action, which informs individuals of the probability of successful satisfaction of future needs. Combined with the criticality of the need, this assessment can provide an estimate of the future level of happiness related to a particular future need. Unlike satisfaction of instant needs, which manifest themselves through distinct actions, *anticipated needs* usually are not time-bound regarding the timing of assessment or execution. Only in the short-term perspective may individuals know the timing of activities aimed at the satisfaction of future needs, *e.g.*, a visit to the doctor or the presentation of a university graduation thesis. Such near-future events may generate separable and instant affective and cognitive responses. In the longer term, individuals do not know the timing or the form of materialization of actions aimed at satisfying future needs.

For instance, individuals commonly do not know how and when they will find a romantic partner or succeed with their career aspirations. Nevertheless, individuals make subjective evaluations of their chances of satisfying such future needs. Such evaluations are performed continuously, covering a substantial stretch of the life horizon, and are repeated for all prominent needs based on personal experience. It is plausible to suggest that throughout need assessment, humans develop a relatively steady and integrated (combining cognitive and affective components) picture of deferred needs and the chances of their satisfaction. This evaluation represents the total level of happiness, which we define as *anticipated happiness*. In predicting future happiness, each need is valued at its relative weight of importance w_i and estimated probability of its satisfaction p_i . For all needs combined, we define *anticipated happiness* as the sum of all estimated probabilities of the satisfaction of future needs:

$$H_a = \sum_{i=1}^{m} p_i w_i \qquad (4)$$

Where:

H_a – the total integrated level of happiness related to *anticipated needs*,

p_i – the estimated probability of fully satisfying need i ($0 \leq p \leq 1$),

w_i – the relative weight of need i ($0 \leq w \leq 1$),

m – the total number of needs.

Anticipated happiness coefficient **H_a** ranges from 0 to 1, where 0 represents complete unhappiness (i.e., no needs are expected to be satisfied) and 1 represents complete happiness (all needs are expected to be fully satisfied). The sum of the relative weights of all needs is equal to 1 (as per Equation 1). For any individual, w_i and p_i are highly subjective, dependent on subjective life circumstances, and influenced by the affective nature of human forecasting, as suggested by Wilson & Gilbert (2003). Humans may also use analytical or intuitive approaches for assessing risks and probabilities of their success, thus, arriving at different conclusions depending on their states of mind (Denes-Raj & Epstein, 1994; Epstein, 1994). Nevertheless, available data suggests that individuals rely on their state of mood only if their mood is pronounced but use other salient information about their life in the absence of pronounced mood states (Schwarz & Strack, 1991). The variable nature of w_i and p_i parameters allows considering happiness in the context of changes in the social environment and personal circumstances. In addition, Equation 4 allows quantifying the well-being of social groups by using statistical data.

The formula for long-term happiness (Equation 4) establishes a link between psychological modeling and decision-making theories, particularly the theory of subjective expected utility developed by Savage (1954) based on the works of Ramsey (2001) and von Neumann (Neumann & Morgenstern, 2007). The subjective expected utility theory incorporates two parameters: the personal utility function and personal probability distribution. Savage (1954) proposes the person making a decision predicts that an uncertain event has possible outcomes *(x_i)*, each with a utility of *u(x_i)*. Then that person's choices can be explained as arising from this utility function, combined with his subjective perception of the probability of each outcome, *P(x_i)*. Accordingly, the subjective expected utility is:

$$U = \sum_{i=1}^{n} P(x_i) u(x_i) \qquad (5)$$

Equation 5 represents the perceived utility of a planned action (an intended action that has not yet occurred), similar to how Equation 4 represents the expectations of a successful outcome of all future actions, both defined and undefined.

Equation 4 introduces new quantitative methods in research on happiness. In technical disciplines, the multiplication of the probability of a specific event (*e.g.*, likelihood of satisfying a need) by the resulting consequences of such event (*e.g.*, the weight of the need) is generally defined as a risk (ISO 45001, n.d.). Usually, a risk has negative connotations as it relates to the probability of an adverse event. Equation 4 gives the probability of the occurrence of a positive event (satisfaction of a need) and therefore defines an opportunity rather than a risk. Risk/opportunity (rewards) analysis is a well-developed knowledge tool widely utilized in business, finance, military planning, and a broad range of technical disciplines.

30 Momentary Happiness *vs.* Anticipated Happiness

Total happiness is a combination of two states, i.e., *momentary happiness* and *anticipated happiness*, which are complementary to each other but self-contained in their origin. The balance between them is unique for each individual and depends on many factors, including social environment, age, gender, life experiences, health, etc. *Momentary happiness* depends on short-term results, while *anticipated happiness* focuses on process and future goals. These approaches represent the two philosophies applied to definitions of success in various social contexts.

The notion of *momentary happiness* and *anticipated happiness* correlates with Zimbardo's works (Zimbardo & Boyd, 1999; D'Alessio et al., 2003) on time perspectives, especially concerning present and future orientated personalities. However, we believe that Zimardo's views are, to some extent, influenced by cultural bias. He claims that:

> Future orientation has been related to many positive consequences for individuals in Western society, such as higher socioeconomic status, superior academic achievement, less sensation seeking, and fewer health risk behaviors. The opposite holds for those with a dominant present orientation, who are seen as at risk for many negative life consequences, among them mental health problems, juvenile delinquency, crime, and addictions, when they

function in a predominantly future-oriented society. (p. 20)

In our opinion, such inequitable preference toward future orientation can be misleading and is not necessarily supported by statistical analysis of the level of happiness across different cultures (Helliwell, Layard, & Sachs, 2017).

Anticipated happiness H_a is defined as the combined probability of satisfying future needs, while variation in *momentary happiness* ΔH_m is defined as the change in the level of happiness resulting from an action; therefore, these two parameters are not necessarily deterministically dependent on each other. Few activities have direct impacts on *anticipated long-term happiness*. Starting a romantic relationship is an example of a long-lasting positive impact of a particular action on long-term happiness. A professional athlete's decision to retire and terminate his sports career is an example of a move with a potentially detrimental impact. More often than not, there is an indirect influence of actions on the H_a value. This effect is enabled through the feedback mechanism when actions affect life experience and the catalog of dominant needs of an individual. Life experience is established based on the results of completed activities and then used as a reference in the risk analysis of satisfaction of future needs.

The interrelation between momentary consequences of actions and acquired personal experience can be complex. For example, an over-caring parent's restrictions on a child may positively impact the child's momentary well-being. At the same time, they can have adverse implications on its long-term happiness through the development of passive behavioral patterns, which adversely affect the child's potential to satisfy specific needs in the future. The *experience & capabilities*

143

database, while accumulating past experiences, also consolidates attitudes, social norms, and cultural predispositions. The individual experience & capabilities database is highly affected by personality traits, as different personality traits lead to different conclusions when evaluating practical experiences. As a result, someone more optimistic in nature may value his chances of satisfying future needs higher than someone who is more pessimistically inclined.

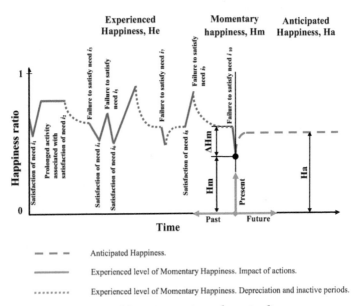

Anticipated Happiness.

Experienced level of Momentary Happiness. Impact of actions.

Experienced level of Momentary Happiness. Depreciation and inactive periods.

Figure 12. A typical happiness time-domain diagram.

Transient actions can also influence long-term well-being by altering the catalog of dominant needs. In that respect, the interrelations between the effect of actions on *momentary* and *anticipated happiness* may be quite intricate. Schwarz & Strack (1991) demonstrate that the same event may influence evaluations of one's life-as-a-whole and assessments of specific domains in opposite directions. For example, an extremely positive event in domain X may induce a good mood, resulting in reports of increased well-being. However, the same event may also increase the standard of comparison used in evaluating domain X, resulting in judgments of decreased satisfaction with this particular domain.

H_m, and H_a parameters can be illustrated by the *time-domain diagram of happiness* (Figure 12), which defines the momentary level of happiness for completed activities and anticipated levels of happiness for outcomes of possible future actions. Experienced *momentary happiness* frequently fluctuates in response to transient life events. A change in happiness levels caused by a particular action/event equals ΔH_m, either positive or negative, and either momentary or long-lasting. The latter would occur in case of a protracted activity, such as attending a sports event or visiting the dentist. As mentioned earlier, people spend most of their time in a semi-active state, such as periods of mind-wandering or recovering from a change in the emotional state on the back of a recently completed action. This condition is illustrated in Figure 12 by the dotted line. Anticipated future happiness H_a, represented by the dashed line, is depicted as having a constant value. However, for some future events (*e.g.,* medical procedures, participation in charity events, or purchasing a house), one can anticipate fluctuations in the future level of happiness as well.

Our proposed concept of two states of happiness, with corresponding coefficients of happiness H_m and H_a, correlates with known distinctions between short-lived happiness and enduring well-being (Davidson & Schuyler, 2015). Overlaps between different theories of happiness are not coincidental as they ultimately originate from or can be related to the *process of human behavior* (Figure 7).

31 Correlation with Other Theories of Happiness

Diener et al. (2002) categorized happiness theories as (1) need and goal satisfaction, (2) process or activity, and (3) genetic and personality predisposition theories. They provided summaries of the three approaches, synopsized in the following paragraphs.

Proponents of need and goal satisfaction theories center on "the idea that the reduction of tensions lead to happiness. Freud's (1933) pleasure principle and Maslow's (1970b) hierarchical needs model represent this approach" (p. 66). Need and goal satisfaction theorists argue that reducing tension and satisfying biological and psychological needs and goals will cause happiness.

The second group, proponents of process or activity theories, consider that engagement in an activity itself provides happiness. Csikszentmihalyi (1975) suggested that people are happier when they engage in interesting activities that match their skill level. He called the state of mind that results from this matching of challenges and skill *flow*. He argued that people who often experience flow tend to be very happy. As such, "both needs theorists and activity theorists argue that subjective well-being will change with the conditions in people's life" (p. 66).

Those who argue for the third approach point to "an element of stability in people's levels of well-being." These theorists argue that stable personality dispositions strongly influence subjective well-being and that "although life events can influence subjective well-being, people eventually adapt to these changes and return to biologically determined *set points* or *adaptation levels* (e.g. Headey & Wearing, 1992)" (p. 67). However, there is little evidence supporting the ideas of complete adaptation to set points irrespective of life circumstances (Helliwell, Layard, & Sachs, 2015). On the other hand, individual-level partial adaptation to life events is a well-known feature of the human psyche. Significant research is being conducted to identify the mechanism of such adaptation (Lyubomirsky, 2011; Sheldon & Lyubomirsky, 2007).

Equations 2, 3, and 4 exemplify the goal satisfaction theory of needs is at the core of our proposed model. At the same time, whilst we describe that happiness is attained through the *process of satisfaction of needs*, it is not accidental that our proposed approach correlates with the *process theories* of happiness as well. These theories are based on the rationale of a balance between individual skills and challenges (Csikszentmihalyi, 1975; Cummins, 2010). Within our model, this balance is achieved through a feedback mechanism between the outcome of actions and the catalog of dominant needs (Figure 7).

We have previously shown that even satisfaction of needs may, in the long run, have a disruptive effect on happiness and create a psychological distortion. Thus, to maintain a state of happiness, it is advantageous to establish a life pattern characterized by a sustainable balance between outcomes of actions and an ever-changing catalog of dominant needs. Hence, within the context of our model, the condition of *flow* occurs when an individual engages in long-lasting and fulfilling activities while maintaining (or enhancing) a desire to continue with these activities through a feedback mechanism. The development of the *process* theories of happiness eventually resulted in the emergence of positive psychology (Seligman & Csikszentmihalyi, 2000). Within the branch of positive psychology, Seligman (2012) devised the concept of PERMA (Positive emotion; Engagement; Relationships; Meaning; Achievement), which transforms a theoretical model into a practical application aiming to enhance the quality of life.

A focus on the long-term balance between needs and outcomes of actions is at the core of the hedonic adaptation theories of happiness. Sheldon and Lyubomirsky (2007) developed the Hedonic Adaptation to Positive and Negative Experience (HAPNE) model. According to Lyubomirsky (2011), adaptation to positive and negative life experiences proceeds via two separate paths. The first path specifies that the stream of positive or negative emotions resulting from the life change (*e.g.*, joy or sadness) may lessen over time, reverting people's happiness levels to their baseline. The second, more counterintuitive path specifies that the stream of positive or negative events resulting from the change may influence people's expectations about their lives positively (or negatively). In such a way, the individual takes circumstances that used to produce happiness for granted or is inured to circumstances that used to produce unhappiness. Both *adaptation paths* of the HAPNE model can be fully integrated into our model of human happiness. The lessening of impacts of actions on *momentary happiness* is taken into account in Equations 2 and 3 for *momentary happiness* by the forgetting factor Y_i. The second component, deflation of repetitive experience, is modeled through a feedback mechanism linking action outcomes to changes in the catalog of dominant needs.

The feedback mechanism results in a situation where successful but repetitive action may diminish the ranking of the need triggering it unless a condition of flow is obtained. Subsequently, devaluing the need relative weight w_i (Equations 2, 3, and 4) would impair increases in *momentary happiness* ΔH_m for repetitive actions aimed at its satisfaction.

In summary, the proposed theory of happiness integrates all three concepts identified by Diener et al. (2002), i.e., *need satisfaction*, *process*, and *individual-level partial hedonic adaptation*. We consider that they represent specific instances of our generalized theory based on the analysis of the *process of satisfaction on needs*. The development of a general concept became possible as we do not attempt to posit a unique standalone theory of happiness but rather derive it from the *process of human behavior* (Figure 7). The idea that multiple theories of happiness can be combined within the premise of a unified concept leads to the conclusion that there is no universal way to enhance happiness but rather numerous paths to its achievement.

While the proposed model of happiness correlates closely to existing theories, it contains several novel and distinguishing features. First, we postulate that any model of happiness should be based on the model of human behavior. Such an approach allows the evaluation of well-being in dynamic settings of a constantly transforming individual acting in ever-changing physical and social environments. Second, we conceptualize that happiness consists separable components associated with specific needs and different time perspectives. All these components of happiness can be derived from the analysis of the behavioral process diagram. Third, the model incorporates the premise of the risk analysis theory. Risk analysis is an advanced analytical method that may bring significant benefits to analyzing and predicting happiness. Lastly, the proposed model is impartial as it does not favor or advocate any specific course of action but instead emphasizes a diversity of strategies for attaining happiness.

Part Nine

The Practicalities of Happiness

32   The Purpose of Life is to Be Happy

A renowned twentieth century writer and philosopher, Ayn Rand (1938), once wrote, "My happiness is not the means to any end. It is the end. It is its own goal. It is its own purpose" (p. 43). Rand's views on the purpose of life later transformed into philosophical and political doctrines. Her ideas became incredibly influential towards the end of the twentieth and beginning of the twenty first centuries. They provided ideological grounds for many prominent politicians in Europe and the United States. One of her close devotees, Alan Greenspan, served as the US Federal Reserve chair and was a key economic policymaker under four presidents from opposing political affiliations. Greenspan's friendship with Ayn Rand had a profound impact on his views as he became a prominent proponent of "laissez-faire" (or, as described by Rand, "full, pure, uncontrolled, unregulated") capitalism.

Rand's ideas also contributed to the development of rational egoism in a philosophical field. While fully concurring with Rand's view on happiness being the sole purpose of life, we reach this postulate from a completely different perspective and fully oppose her keynote conclusion, namely, Rand's condemnation of ethical altruism as incompatible with the requirements of human life (Badhwar & Long, 2020). Our premise is as follows - life is a sequence of activities, and life is successful if activities satisfy the needs (wants, wishes) that trigger them. Satisfied needs generate happiness, and thus, the purpose of life is to be happy. We see happiness as the sole criterion for a successful life and fully concur with Rand's views on happiness being "its own purpose." However, we disagree with her conception shared by many philosophers and laypeople that human needs are intrinsically egoistic. This standpoint is not true; egoism and altruism are coexisting sides of the human psyche. Their combination is evident for humans and animals and manifests in offspring caring, bravery in fighting for the group's interests, and even self-sacrifice. To be happy, one has to satisfy both egoistic and altruistic needs, the balance between which varies and depends on the individual's life circumstances.

33 Why We are Always on Edge

The human psyche is an intrinsically unstable system that requires constant intervention. An individual always has something to deal with: a shortage of resources or skills, conflicts at work or home, unfriendly encounters with strangers, the lack of emotional support, health scares, insufficient career growth, poor examination grades, gloomy political news, and economic threats, among others. Humans live in a constant unbalance, the main reason for which is a mismatch between needs and skills. Often, individuals find themselves in situations where available knowledge and capabilities are insufficient to fully cater to the satisfaction of the never-ending cascade of needs they experience. Paradoxically, even satisfaction triggers dissatisfaction, in line with Rolling Stone's famous musical verse, "I can't get no satisfaction, cause I try, and I try." Even when a particular need is successfully satisfied, it still has the potential to throw the psyche out of balance, as its satisfaction "frees up space" for a new need, and the individual would have to start working all over again on attending to the newly aroused need.

This disbalance originates from objective tensions engulfing the worlds within and outside us. These tensions of different natures result from conflicts between the primary perspectives of our existence:

- Body and mind,
- An individual and his environment,
- An individual and another individual,
- An individual and a group,
- A group and another group.

In most circumstances, humans possess a sufficient toolbox of skills to mitigate and eventually resolve encountered tensions; however, much physical and psychological effort may be required. On the one hand, such strains cause us distress, but on the other, they are also the sole triggers of our actions, hence, are the ultimate reasons for us to live. In other words, without distress, trials, and tribulations, life would have no meaning.

34   Today's and Tomorrow's Happiness are not Alike

Happiness is the result of satisfaction of needs achieved through actions. The level of success of efforts converts into a sense of momentary happiness. However, individuals only fully concentrate on the activities at hand around half the time (Killingsworth & Gilbert, 2010). For the remainder, we typically find ourselves at least partially engaged in "stimulus-independent thought" or "mind wandering." Perhaps, the American duo Simon and Garfunkel alluded to this in their *The Only Living Boy In New York* lyrics: "Half of the time we're gone, but we don't know where, and we don't know where."

But even in this state, our brain does not change its "modus operandi" as it is "wired" to do only one thing: cater to our needs. The difference is that when our minds wander, we are preoccupied not with momentary needs but with future or anticipated needs that manifest through dreams, aspirations, and a sense of inevitability of the future. The brain similarly works on future anticipated needs as on momentary needs, the only difference being that the action implementation phase is not present; hence, our responses end with intent and risk assessment. The results of these assessments provide the basis for our estimate of how successful we would be in satisfying anticipated needs. This estimate entails another dimension of happiness, i.e., anticipated happiness.

Momentary and anticipated components of happiness are complementary but self-contained in their origin. Total happiness is a combination of the two. The balance between the two types of happiness is unique for each individual and depends on many factors, including social environment, age, gender, life experiences, health, etc. Momentary happiness depends on short-term results, while anticipated happiness focuses more on behavioral processes and future goals.

35   To Be Happy - Satisfy Your Needs

Happiness is an individual's cognitive and affective evaluation of their life. Life is a sequence of actions aimed at the satisfaction of needs. Notwithstanding this multitude of vibrant enlightenments, the main behavioral principles of happiness can be derived from the definition that "happiness is an individual's cognitive and affective evaluation of their life," which translates into the following five governing behavioral traits (Diener et al., 2002, Diener et al., 2009) for the attainment of happiness:

- Frequent encounters of positive experiences,
- Increased magnitude of positive experiences,
- Rare encounters of negative experiences,
- Curtailed magnitude of negative experiences,
- A positive view of one's future.

The first four behavioral traits predominantly enhance momentary happiness, while the last one primarily enhances anticipated happiness. Negative and positive experiences are itemized separately because they have dissimilar impacts on the human psyche and do not simply negate each other. That is why losing and finding the same thing are not equally weighted events of opposite signs. All so-called "recipes" for attaining happiness fall into one or several referenced categories. The five behavioral traits provide a relatively straightforward perspective on happiness, and in their simplicity, allow to some extent, to untangle and demystify the subject by recognizing that all life strategies for happiness attainment stem from these five essential traits.

Whilst originating from a few well-defined behavioral traits, happiness is a complex phenomenon accounting for both momentary and anticipated perspectives and consisting of individualized components associated with separable needs. Needs are satisfied through actions executed following a standard process of human behavior composed of multiple features, each of which can also affect happiness (Figure 7). Hence, there are many paths to attaining happiness, and there is no one-size-fits-all solution. Examples of common happiness enhancement strategies include:

- Improve specific skills to increase the likelihood of satisfaction of needs,
- Increase frequency of engagement in desirable activities to increase the frequency of positive affect,
- Withdraw from activities causing distress,
- Lower ambitions to improve chances of satisfaction of needs,
- Increase the complexity of challenges to increase the magnitude of positive affect,
- Concentrate on satisfying only a limited number of needs,
- Avoid challenges to minimize negative affect,
- Establish a long-lasting balance between challenges and skills (e.g., attain the condition of a prolonged sense of "flow"),
- Develop personality traits that enhance a positive life attitude and self-confidence,
- Passively hope for positive outcomes (e.g., expect luck).

Choosing a specific happiness strategy depends on life circumstances, such as one's general experiences, social and physical environments, health, age, and gender. Some happiness strategies can be controversial, such as religious asceticism or activities where one engages in extreme risk-taking. In the case of religious asceticism, happiness is attained through willful obliteration of needs that are otherwise considered essential (e.g., family living, wealth, social aspirations) with an aim to increase the frequency and magnitude of positive affects and improve the chances of satisfaction of fewer needs and wishes (e.g., religious worshiping, righteous living). This is an example of a strategy when happiness is attained by reducing the variety and complexity of needs by prioritizing only a small number of them. Similarly, extreme risk-taking also aims at increasing the frequency and magnitude of positive affects – but it is achieved through a contrary course by deliberately complicating life circumstances, by seeking challenging and eventful environments, such as in the examples of rock climbing or skydiving. Some strategies may fail or be counterproductive. For example, a withdrawal from social engagements can be someone's strategy to reduce the frequency of negative affect in response to dissatisfaction with certain types of group interactions, which may cause social anxiety and isolation in the long term.

All stages in the *process of human behavior* (Figure 7) may impact the state of happiness. Missed or incorrectly interpreted signals, inadequately assessed risks, poorly constructed plans, or faultily executed actions may influence happiness levels. Performance efficiency in each behavioral process phase is affected by an individual's physical, psychological, and cognitive capabilities. For a standalone action, taken in isolation from personal disposition and life circumstances, physical and cognitive skills appear to have a decisive role in forging success and happiness.

However, subjectively, success is always calibrated against an individual's needs. Identification of priority needs, which are manifested through wants, goals, aspirations, and dreams, plays a crucial role in defining an individual's happiness. The importance of this factor is especially evident in the case of *anticipated needs*, for which the execution stage does not exist (as the need is foreseen, but no immediate action is undertaken), while signal detection, signal assessment, and planning phases are significantly subdued. In this case, the likelihood of future success is determined primarily by defining dominant needs, and secondly by chances of their satisfaction, as estimated through risk assessment. One's selection of priority needs has a dramatic effect on life satisfaction. The highest levels of evaluation of life quality are attained not necessarily when needs are worthy or abilities are potent but when needs correlate with the capabilities required to achieve them. Fine-tuning the balance between needs and skills is one of the main functions of the human psyche.

Happiness strategies are defined by the five traits and implemented through the primary components of the human behavior process. Although the total number of combinations of these factors is considerable, it is not unlimited, which makes a future full listing of happiness strategies plausible.

36   The Happiness Paradox

In 1958, American ethologist, John B. Calhoun, started a series of experiments in which he researched the impact of abundance on the behavior of mice and rats. He created "rat utopias" or "mouse paradise" by providing unlimited resources, such as water, food, and protection from predators, disease, and weather. In doing so, he established conditions enabling unfettered population growth within limited confines of experimental facilities. Experiments ended with devastating results for the communities of animals:

> Many [female rats] were unable to carry pregnancy to full term or to survive delivery of

their litters if they did. An even greater number, after successfully giving birth, fell short in their maternal functions. Among the males the behavior disturbances ranged from sexual deviation to cannibalism and from frenetic overactivity to a pathological withdrawal from which individuals would emerge to eat, drink and move about only when other members of the community were asleep. The social organization of the animals showed equal disruption. (Calhoun, 1970, p. 54)

Calhoun described the collapse in behavior leading eventually to the population's extinction as "spiritual death" and attributed it to the effects of overcrowding (Calhoun, 1973). Nonetheless, the experiments continue to cause discourse, and some researchers, including Garnett (2008), believe that moral decay resulted not from density, but excessive social interaction.

We want to offer another alternative view on the outcome of Calhoun's experiments. If the essence of the experiments was modeling "the paradise," then their outcome must represent precisely that – the impact of absolute satisfaction of needs on an individual's living and a social group's functioning. From this vantage point, the behavioral collapse was triggered by the conditions of the "paradise" rather than overcrowding. Could it be that it was not an experiment on modeling the effects of overcrowding, as initially intended, but rather a simulation of conditions of absolute satisfaction of needs, equating, according to our views, to the state of complete happiness? Animals had all their needs intrinsically satisfied, thus, impeding their motivational drives and making obsolete basic behavioral mechanisms aimed at the satisfaction of needs.

Perhaps, the encountered conditions rendered their core behavioral instincts worthless and caused their individual and social demise.

We are not trying to conclude on the fundamentals of human behavior based on the outcome of simple experiments conducted on animals. We rather provide food for reflection concerning hypothetical cases of entirely unhappy and totally happy individuals. In the former case, none of an individual's needs are satisfied, and a person is utterly unhappy. Although this is purely a hypothetical situation, for all the practical reasons, this individual would have been dead because his need for oxygen would not have been satisfied, among others. But let us consider a situation at the opposite end of the happiness spectrum, i.e., a person is absolutely happy, meaning that all their needs are continuously satisfied. Strangely enough, this person would not have a reason to live either. Living is actioning, and all actions are triggered by unsatisfied needs. If all needs are satisfied, a person has no reason to act and, hence, to live. The happiness paradox is that the most dreadful and the most desirable states of the human psyche are equally detrimental to it!

We have to conclude that the degree of unhappiness, i.e., the subsistence of unsatisfied needs, is beneficial for an individual and is required for their further development, perhaps, even existence. One may speculate that the entire progress of humankind originates from unhappiness. It does not necessarily imply that continuous complete satisfaction of needs is detrimental, but rather that the whole current arrangement of life in general and psyche, in particular, is not set for the conditions of abundance. It can be argued that the sole purpose of life is the satisfaction of needs in the state of a shortage of resources. Thus, the continuous absolute satisfaction of needs would require reformatting the basic principles of living, including the redefinition of its purpose.

37   Why the Rich and Famous are Miserable

After Michael Jackson had released the best-selling album of all time, "Thriller," in 1982, he decided that his next album, which became "Bad," should outsell his previous record. To help him achieve this goal, he started putting up signs and notes around his houses that urged him to work harder and harder to outdo his previous efforts. As it would turn out, he failed - "Bad" sold tens of millions fewer copies than "Thriller." Nevertheless, "Bad" was a musical masterpiece in the top 15 bestselling music albums of all time. Undoubtedly, Michael Jackson's never-ending race for greater success and continued public recognition would be one of the leading factors in his tragic death in 2009 from a cardiac arrest caused by overdosing on medications. Despite his enormous accomplishments, Michael Jackson was not a happy man in life. There are many other examples of successful people from diverse backgrounds and professions; music artists, prosperous entrepreneurs, and record-beating athletes who later became disillusioned with their efforts and found themselves in difficult life circumstances.

The underlying reason for this apparent unhappiness is that achieved goals tend to self-destruct. As the need associated with a specific purpose is satisfied, it leaves a void in the psyche, which requires it to be filled by another need. The human psyche works so that one's "basket of needs" is continuously replenished as satisfying needs "open up space" for new needs to rise and take root. In a perfect world, the recently arisen needs would match available skills, but what happens if the new needs require a new set of skills for their attainment, which is not at hand? An example is an Olympic champion who's about to retire from sports. When encountered with a new and unfamiliar life situation outside professional sports that requires entirely new competencies, they may emotionally feel as if their previous achievements were done for nothing, leaving them "emptyhanded" at the end of their career. Consider also what happens to an individual who is "addicted" to recreating their previous success and fails to do it. They may end up in a predicament where it is not them who control the goals, but their goals have "taken control" over them, as was ultimately the case with Michael Jackson.

A "hard" goal that is connected to a rigid and precisely defined personal key performance indicator should, in some circumstances, be considered "dangerous" and approached "with care" to avoid damaging the psychological balance of an individual upon the achievement of that goal. Preferably, the "hard" goal should be seen as a destination paired with a "soft" goal which is the "journey" to that destination. In that case, even a failure to reach the destination does not negate the completed stretch of the journey. And if the destination is reached, the journey may go on and continue further. In Michael Jackson's case, the destination was to be the best artist in the world, and the journey was to bring joy to people through music. The artist ultimately became exhausted by his goals while failing to enjoy the journey of his achievements.

There is a thin line between goals as a motivator and goals as a disruptor of the psyche. Hard goals are often praised and deservingly so. However, they are only good if accompanied by a sense of direction, which exhibits its guidance both ahead and beyond the moment of achievement. The ideal balance between soft and hard goals is not a given, and varies depending on personal circumstances, social norms, and attitudes.

38   The Journey and the Destination

We have established that satisfaction of needs through successful completion of actions enhances happiness; the better the results of undertaken actions, the happier the individual. At the same time, the successful satisfaction of a need negates it and does not guarantee the preservation of happiness. We also know that only around half the time, we concentrate entirely on the activities at hand (Killingsworth & Gilbert, 2010). During the remaining time, our minds partly wander, actively assessing future needs, which do not require immediate action but for which we seek confidence to be able to address them when the time comes. From these perspectives, the results of actions do not matter per se. They might provide some sort of statistical reassurance, but nothing more. What matters is that we have sound routines and methods that increase our chances of success in the future. In that regard, even a failure is manageable if one knows how to resolve it or acquire such knowledge.

The question is, what should one concentrate on – the achievement in itself or the process of achievement? In reality, it is always a combination of the two, though often with a distinct preference or tilt toward one or the other. A hypothetical slave-owner, computer programmer, professional sportsman, student, or parent, may all have their specific preferences and rationale for selecting one of these two strategies. The choice is not so trivial, as it implies a commitment to a particular life strategy and must consider the surrounding setting, the task at hand, personal traits, societal expectations, age, and many other factors.

We believe humankind transition from goal-orientated living to process-orientated living. This gradual and prolonged shift is due to happiness being accomplished not only upon any achievement (short-lived satisfaction) but also through the process of achievement (prolonged satisfaction). At home, school, and work, hard goals defined through grades, key performance indicators, and fixed milestones will give way to values, self-motivation, and adaptable planning. A former military officer and US President, Dwight Eisenhower, once said, "planning is everything, the plan is nothing." With a touch of exaggeration, we rephrase it to a proposition that "the process of achieving is everything, the achievement is nothing."

39   Dreams Matter

Nowadays, few would dispute that dreams and aspirations are important for human motivation and character building. Nevertheless, dreams are often assigned to such domains as youthfulness, work incentive programs, and novel writing. Indeed, there is no immediate return on dreaming. However, it is essential to remember that around half the time, our minds are engaged in assessing future anticipated activities, and dreams, aspirations, and life planning account for the anticipated happiness component in the overall realm of happiness. If the anticipated happiness related to the satisfaction of future needs is low, then regardless of the fulfillment of current needs, the person might remain unhappy. This state represents an adverse condition of the human psyche. Individuals and society should regard dreams, aspirations, and hopes as vital factors of subjective well-being and consider them thoroughly in parenting, education, the work environment, and policymaking.

40   The Truth Behind Happy Children

Conventional psychology teaches that reconnecting with your "inner child" can help foster well-being and bring lightness to life. The general idea of the so-called "inner child" is based around connecting with past experiences and memories of innocence, playfulness, and creativity, along with a high hope for the future. Such teachings have almost become universal mantras, at least in some circles.

Two particular attributes of happiness differentiate childhood. Firstly, due to limited social responsibilities, a child has fewer concerns about the future and primarily lives in the present – a very effective happiness trait. The second feature is less obvious, and therefore, less recognized. Due to a perpetual intense physical, psychological, and social evolvement, a child constantly faces the emergence of new needs, which demand the continuous acquisition of new knowledge and skills. In reality, the effortless, sometimes seemingly non-essential, childish time passing is the most demanding and productive phase of a lifetime regarding the formation of the mind and psyche.

Children's development starts with a blank page. They must learn absolutely everything from scratch, including what colors different objects are, what taste they have, how to interpret speech, how to control their own body, how to fight, how to flee, how to win friends, and how to influence people, among others. A baby making cooing sounds and clumsily jerking his limbs, a toddler aimlessly running on a playground or staring through a window to no apparent avail, a child throwing a tantrum – all these are acts of intense learning, advancement of social skills, calibration of own body and mind. In the acquisition of experience, the outcome of these seemingly mindless and sometimes annoying to others activities is equivalent to relentless training and concentrated studying performed later in life at a great physical and emotional expense. By the end of childhood, individuals acquire most of the knowledge they'll ever have. Learning obtained through school and university pales compared to the vast knowledge gained in childhood.

Moreover, the skills acquired in childhood are tremendously valuable, the return on efforts is immense, and lessons learned are applied almost instantly. This constant learning is a very gratifying process, to the extent that it could be said that children live in a state of supercharged flow. Flow is a state of the psyche during which a deep-rooted balance between a specific critical need and the set of skills allowing its satisfaction is activated. In the case of children, they enter into the state of flow while dealing not with a particular need but with an extensive range of needs, and not just one set of skills, but with a wide range of skills, all of which possess immense importance. Another unique feature of the childhood supercharge flow is that the skills are not simply applied but developed in real-time to balance the arousal of needs. For an adult entering a state of flow, is a unique occurrence, but for a child, it is the natural way of being. Whether it is possible to connect with one's inner child – we say it is viable, as far as attempting to live "in the present," though not easily attainable. It is much more challenging to reach a state of supercharged flow, close to impossible, though attempting it can be rewarding on its own.

41   Flow

Flow is one of the few proven conditions enhancing happiness. Flow is traditionally defined as the mental state in which a person experiences total immersion and enjoyment whilst performing a particular activity. Flow is characterized by complete absorption in what one does, which transforms one's perception of time. According to Mihaly Csikszentmihalyi (1990), who coined the notion of flow, it occurs because all of a person's attention in the flow state is on the task at hand, so there is no more attention to be allocated. In our opinion, the traditional conceptualization of flow does not fully reveal its underlying causes.

Several things must happen for flow to occur. These include the appearance of a critical need, a balance between skills and the need, and continuous regeneration of the need. Until now, the last point has not been duly considered in the concept of flow, and we believe it is an essential precondition for the flow state to occur, distinguishing it from other psychological conditions. Normally, satisfaction of a need negates it, as the need dissipates after it has been satisfied. But this does not happen in a state of flow when the need is preserved by the action, allowing repetitive regeneration of positive sensations associated with satisfaction of the need in question.

Contrary to the conventional view, we do not include any references to the time aspect in the conditions of flow. We purposefully do not refer to the "activity at hand" or the loss of "sense of time." Regarding the time perspective, we conceptualize that flow can occur over the short term and be intense or long-lasting and more moderate in sensation. In the latter case, the condition of being in the flow state is extended and concurrent to other psychological experiences; it is typically less intense but still rewarding. Hence, we apply the characterization of flow, not only to the description of activities at hand, but also to longer-lasting psychological experiences like satisfaction experienced from stimulating work, romantic relationships, or absorbing hobbies. These psychological states associated with the long-lasting recurring needs generating positive sensations can also be described as passions. The common characteristic for all occurrences of flow (short-term experience) and passion (long-lasting experience) is that action through the satisfaction of the need does not negate the need but rather preserves it. The classification into short-term and prolonged types of flow correlates well with our concept of momentary and anticipated perspectives of happiness.

42   Suicide is the Elimination of Needs

At first glance, suicides would contradict the general law of preservation. However, the laws are not imposed upon humans but enabled through the universal course of behavior, representing a process of satisfaction of needs. Paradoxically, suicide can be viewed as a path towards eliminating unhappiness by eliminating the needs causing it, although achieved through extremely drastic measures by the termination of life itself. Situations leading to suicides are characterized by overwhelming domination of a particular set of needs that the individual cannot satisfy. Such dominance can occur short term or be prolonged. The former is typically caused by an acute detrimental change of life circumstances, such as the abrupt end of romantic relations. The latter is more gradual in development and can be exemplified by cases of severe depression or chronic physical pain.

The suicide phenomenon also sheds light on the relationship between the body and the mind, as the latter becomes increasingly dominant over the body. Most suicides are attributed to upheavals of the mind, especially considering that the prerogative of making the final decision always belongs to the mind.

43   Flow, Passion, Panic, and Depression

It happened when I accidentally separated from the group during a hike in the woods – I suddenly realized that I had no clue where I was and where I should go. I was instantly overwhelmed by a wave of fear and senselessly rushed into the forest's deepness without any idea of where I was going and without any attempt to reason the situation. My need to find a safe way out was overpowering – and as I felt utterly helpless, I lost all my bearings and panicked.

Panic is a sudden sensation of intense fear accompanied by anxiety and agitation. In the panic state, behavior defies the principles of reasoning and becomes disordered and detached from reality. We conceive panic is somewhat similar to short-term flow but of the opposite kind – a type of "anti-flow." Accordingly, the framework for analyzing states of panic and short-term flow can be the same, as both arise from similar conditions. Both states represent a response to a vital need. For short-term flow, an individual's skills fully balance their needs. Conversely, in a state of panic, the individual's skills do not match their immediate needs at all. There are no previous experiences, memory references, or knowledge on how to handle, curtail, or at least control the encountered needs. In both cases, actions reinforce needs. In a flow state, the need is preserved to allow for the continuation of positive sensations; in the panic state, the need is preserved because the action, being completely irrelevant, fails to address the need, and the need ultimately remains.

In the state of panic, the individual does not simply cease to act due to their inability to address the need, but on the contrary, proceeds with action; however, the actions fail entirely to address the needs. An individual in the panic state still "realizes" they have to act and to do so in proportion to the urgency of the need but disregards the logic of the situation entirely.

Concerning depression, we conceive it is akin to long-lasting flow but of the opposite sign – a long-lasting "anti-flow." In commonality to the condition of the long-lasting flow, it arises as a reaction to a critical need. The difference is, in the case of depression, a vital need remains chronically unsatisfied. Usually, a person is equipped with at least some skills to initiate an action required to accomplish a need. But there are cases where a person lacks particular experiences and skills. Such situations may result from deficiencies in personality development or changes in circumstances, which actualize new

171

needs for which an individual's psyche is not fully equipped. In many instances, the individual may attempt to develop new skills, but again there would be cases when such required adjustments fail. The need will remain preserved due to the failure to address it while preventing the diversion of attention to other needs. A chronic long-term lack of satisfaction of a critical need adversely affects an individual's subjective well-being and may cause depression. When an individual is unable to satisfy a prominent need, the psyche seeks other ways of rectifying the situation. An individual may opt to withdraw from detrimental activities or try to delay them, which may negatively impact the satisfaction of other needs. For example, an imbalance in a particular social skill may cause a person to avoid social encounters, which in turn may reinforce distress through the sense of social exclusion or due to the critical reaction of peers; therefore, further escalating the negative trend.

We conceive that the main pre-conditions of depression are: the existence of a prolonged essential need; chronic mismatch between the skills one has and the skills required to attain the need; and continuous preservation of the need due to an inability to act upon it. These conditions symmetrically oppose the ones of long-lasting flow (love or passion). In the case of long-lasting flow (love or passion), need and experience are fully balanced; in the opposite case of depression, need and experience are profoundly out of sync.

In its origin, the state of depression has similarities with the state of panic. The difference between these two states is that panic is an intense but short-lasting and entirely overpowering state caused by an imbalance between need and skill over the short term. In the case of depression, an imbalance of need and skill occurs over the long term, is more moderately exhibited, and develops in parallel with other life experiences.

Depression is a complex phenomenon that we cannot claim to have provided a comprehensive concept, but the proposed model offers a plausible and intriguing perspective.

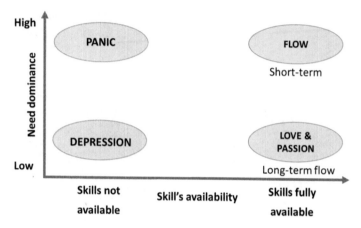

Figure 13. Psychological states associated with recurring dominant needs.

We presented a unified viewpoint on psychological states such as panic, depression, flow, and love/passion (long-term flow). These four extreme states of the human psyche associated with recurring needs differ in intensity, duration, and type of affect. Individual experiences in normal life are situated within these boundaries and balance between the extremes. Transient experiences are less profound, with subdued levels of need dominance and intermediate rates of competency. We hypothesize that if states of flow, panic, love/passion, and depression were plotted on a schematic of need dominance vs. skill availability (Figure 13), they would define the contour of the overall field of the human psyche associated with recurring needs. An artistic impression of the same diagram is presented in Figure 14.

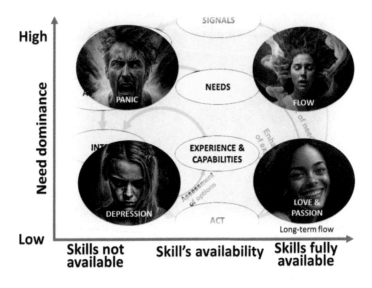

Figure 14. A field of psychological states (an artistic impression).

Part Ten

Towards Unification of Psychology

44   A Model of Unified Psychology

Previously, we formulated (Kopsov, 2021b) a threefold challenge facing modern psychology: (1) a transformation from observations to modeling, (2) a shift from "using words" to "using numbers," and (3) tackling the fundamental questions of human existence (i.e., meaning of life, attainment of happiness, relation between mind and body). Further, we presented a new model of unified psychology and then examined how it addressed the issues mentioned above.

The behavioral process diagram (Figure 7) represents a coherent system of interconnected elements related to various components of the human psyche. Our premise is that if the psychological perspectives can be correlated to the specific elements of the behavioral process, they can then be united under a single system. In this setting, the behavioral schematic plays the role of a common framework linking fragmented concepts. To implement this proposition, we assess the primary attributes of the main psychology perspectives (behavioral, biological, cognitive, humanistic, psychodynamic, and social) in the context of the behavioral process.

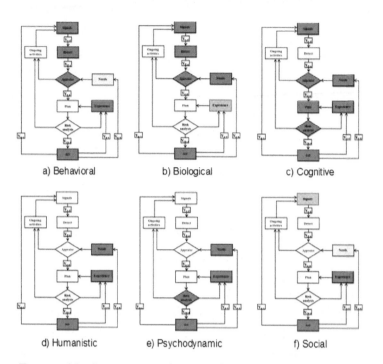

Figure 15. Projection of psychology perspectives on the diagram of human behavior. (Behavioral process components corresponding to primary attributes of perspectives are highlighted in red).

To illustrate the outlined method, we may consider, for instance, the psychodynamic perspective. Its projection onto the behavioral process schematic will reveal the following correlations: "interpersonal relations" in psychoanalysis correlate to the "act" step of the diagram; the "defenses" attribute relates to the "risk analysis" step; the combination of "perception of self, others" and "childhood experience" correspond to the "experience & capabilities" block; and "sexual desires" are addressed by the "needs" block of the diagram. The same process is applied to all analyzed perspectives, and identified correlations are summarized in Figure 15 and Table 4. Figure 15 depicts the six versions of the process schematic, one for each psychological perspective. It should be noted that the process diagrams shown in Figures 7 and 13 are the same and differ only in the design style. If a primary attribute of a psychological perspective correlates to an element of the behavioral process diagram, this element is colored. If the correlation is partial, then the element is shaded. The components of the diagram with no or insignificant correlations are left blank.

Table 4 provides correlations of psychological perspectives with the two core types of elements of the behavioral schematic, i.e., the "main process steps" and "regulating blocks." When a primary attribute of a psychological perspective correlates to a component of the schematic, it is marked "Yes," and if the correlation is in part, it is marked as "partial."

Table 4. Primary attributes of psychology perspectives in relation to components of the behavioral process diagram.

Perspective		Behavioral process components					
		Behavioral	Biological	Cognitive	Human-istic	Psycho-dynamic	Social
Behavioral process		Figure 2a	Figure 2b	Figure 2c	Figure 2d	Figure 2e	Figure 2f
Type	Element						
Stimulus	Signal	Yes	Yes	Yes	-	-	Partly
Step	Detect	Yes	Yes	-	-	-	-
Step	Appraisal	Yes	Yes	Yes	-	-	-
Step	Intent	-	-	Yes	-	-	-
Step	Risk analysis	-	-	Yes	-	Yes	-
Response	Act	Yes	Yes	Yes	Yes	Yes	Yes
Regulating block	Needs	-	Yes	Yes	Yes	Yes	-
Regulating block	Experience, Capabilities	Yes	Partly	Yes	Yes	Yes	Yes

The paired attributes of the perspectives and behavioral diagram modules are listed hereunder in the format "perspective component" – "behavioral process diagram component:"

Behavioral: Stimulus – Signal; Response – Act; Signal Assessment – Detect & Apprise; Adaptation – Experience & Capabilities.

Biological: Stimulus – Signal; Response – Act; Perception of Sensation – Detect & Apprise; Genetics – Experience & Capabilities (partial); Mental Processing – Apprise & Needs & Experience & Capabilities (partial).

Cognitive: Stimulus – Signal; Response – Act; Perception – Apprise, Problem Solving – Needs & Intent & Risk Analysis; Memory – Experience & Capabilities; Learning – Experience & Capabilities; Beliefs – Experience & Capabilities.

Humanistic: Gratification – Act; Need – Needs; Growth – Experience & Capabilities; Autonomy – Experience & Capabilities.

Psychodynamic: Interpersonal Relations – Act; Defenses – Risk Analysis; Perception of Self, Others – Experience & Capabilities; Childhood Experience – Experience & Capabilities; Sexual Desires – Needs.

Social: Social Interactions – Signal (partial) & Act; Beliefs, Attitudes, Norms – Experience & Capabilities.

Table 4 demonstrates that biological, behavioral, and cognitive perspectives cover most of the elements of the behavioral schematic. No wonder some scholars have considered these perspectives to be eligible in their own merit for the role of a unified theory of psychology. Humanistic, psychodynamic, and social perspectives have lower correlations with the schematic. This finding is unsurprising in that, while they provide a deep insight into the human psyche, they fall short of offering a universal model of human behavior. The conceived methodology can similarly be applied to other perspectives not covered in the analysis.

The diagram of the human behavior process sufficiently represents and captures the primary attributes of the analyzed psychological perspectives. It opens a path toward a balanced integration of research conducted based on different premises. The framework of the behavioral process allows us to derive correlations between various perspectives, determine their overlapping and complementary features, and identify "missing links" within each perspective, i.e., lacking components. The proposed formal schematic can then be used as a model for each specific perspective as well as for unified psychology in general. As a result, what were fragmented psychological perspectives can now be established as complementing parts of a single body of psychology rather than a plethora of contending schools of thought.

The proposed methodology is equally valid for unifying divisions within individual perspectives. For example, some proponents of behaviorism consider that [behaviorist] psychology consists of two sciences. One is experimental psychology or stimulus-response psychology which connects behavior to encountered situations and previous experiences. The other is correlational (psychometric) psychology, which relates behavior to various properties (characteristics, attributes) of organisms such as race, sex, age, social class, physiological condition, and psychological traits (Cronbach, 1957; Kimble, 1996).

We believe that an analytical approach when psychometric and experimental parameters are considered individually is somewhat plausible, but claiming that they are separate sciences is a gross error. Moreover, distinguishing independent behavioral variables as present situations, previous experiences, and psychometric parameters is counterproductive because it ignores their interconnection and overlooks a variable of human needs. This kind of simplification led to the regrettable demise of behaviorism, which used to be the dominant school of psychology. Contrarily, the behavioral process diagram (Figure 7) shows that experimental and psychometric psychologies are integral parts of a single concept. Within the diagram, the "encountered situations" are represented by "signals" and "previous experiences" together with psychometric parameters modeled by the "experience and capabilities" module.

181

Figure 15 does not comprehensively describe correlations between various perspectives and the behavioral process. Its primary intent is to demonstrate the method of projection of psychological perspectives into the process diagram. Our analysis is relatively high level; a more detailed evaluation is likely to reveal more nuanced interrelations between the behavioral schematic and psychological perspectives. Their integration cannot be mechanical; the diagram elements are multi-componential in that they contain physical, biological, and consciousness aspects, which can be sensibly combined but not mechanistically fused. Behavioral model elements may need to be ranked (or prioritized) regarding their relevancy to particular perspectives as primary, secondary, etc. We already apply this approach in our assessment. For example, correlation with the "signals" behavioral module in the case of the social perspective is classed as "partial" (Figure 15f). The correlation is partial because this psychological perspective considers mainly the social type of signals out of the full spectrum of signals absorbed by an individual. It is plausible that the behavioral model will continue to evolve through the partitioning of its elements; for example, needs and experiences can be divided into subelements or categories, covering separate physical, biological, mental, and social dimensions.

We categorize the components of the behavioral schematic into four primary types: main process steps, regulating blocks, feedback loops, and transfer functions. We have deliberately limited the scope of our assessment to main process steps and regulating modules. Feedback loops and transfer functions are left out to "streamline" the methodology at its conception. However, further enhancements of the model of unified psychology will likely include all types of components of the behavioral process.

45 Persistent Questions of Psychology

Along with philosophers, psychologists have a full mandate to study metaphysical aspects and the eternal questions of human living. We recently noted (Kopsov, 2020a) that "whilst philosophers may approach such subjects as "fundamental truths," psychologists have the advantage of studying humans in real life and observe first-hand how individuals and societies transform throughout the flow of time." A credible paradigm of psychology must offer a roadmap and, where possible, provide tangible reflections on fundamental issues, also defined by Hergenhahn (2008) as the persistent questions of psychology. Accordingly, our response to these questions is presented further and summarized in Table 5.

What is the nature of human nature?

Human nature is determined by the laws of the preservation of life and the mind. The main principles of human behavior are defined by the process diagram of human behavior (Figure 7).

How are the mind and the body related?

The mind emerges from the evolutionary development of the body for the purpose of enhancement of organism preservation. Eventually, the mind becomes so distinguishable that it can be viewed almost as "extrinsic" to the body. Nevertheless, the mind is rooted within the body, affected by the body, and to a large extent controls the body's well-being. The mind often acts in a supervening manner to the body and sometimes negates it by advancing its priorities at the expense of bodily preservation and reproduction. The interrelations between body and mind are both complementary and adversarial as they have separate dominant needs and pursue different priorities in evolutionary development.

To what extent are the causes of human behavior innate as opposed to experiential?

The causes of human behavior are both innate and experiential. The proposed theory defines the main steps and factors of the processes of human behavior. It explains interrelations between signals, needs, and experience, and by doing so, provides a platform for further studies and analysis of the innate and experimental causes of behavior.

To what extent, if any, is human behavior freely chosen as opposed to completely determined?

All objects and systems forming the universe known to us are intrinsically reactive. Human behavior is inherently reactive too, i.e., humans react to signals and do so according to a predetermined procedure. The freedom of human behavior originates from the ability to select and influence circumstances generating signals, which they react to. A significant portion of signals triggering behavior is of psychological nature, and in that regard, human behavior is also at least partially determined by an individual.

Is there some vital (nonmaterial) force in human nature that prevents a completely mechanistic explanation of human behavior?

The original premise of the new paradigm arises from the materialistic view of human nature. It does not include nonmaterial forces. However, our theory of evolution behavior predicts the possible emergence, and therefore, the possible existence of other forms of nature, which may be perceived as nonmaterial. Hence, though nonmaterial factors are not considered, their possible influence is not entirely discarded.

To what extent do the irrational aspects of human nature (for example, emotions, intuitions, and instincts) contribute to human behavior, as opposed to the rational aspects?

The proposed theory does not explicitly address the irrational aspects of human nature as the derived classification of components defining the process of human behavior is relatively high-level. The model provides the basis for further enhancement to account for the role and place of subconsciousness, emotions, etc.

How are humans related to nonhuman animals?

The theory does not distinguish between humans and animals. It approaches the differences between them as quantitative, not qualitative. At one stage, inevitably, quantitative differences transform into new qualities. Has this transformation already happened within the evolution from animals to modern humans? The theory does not give a conclusive answer to this question but provides the basis for further analysis.

What is the origin of human knowledge?

Knowledge is the combination of experience and reasoning. The question about the origin of human knowledge must be considered together with another commonly overlooked question: "What is the purpose of human knowledge?" The purpose of knowledge is to facilitate the future orientation of behavior in order to enhance self-preservation. Knowledge is information and as such, is not a unique prerogative of humans or animals but a common feature of animate life and inanimate substances. Human knowledge represents an interim phase in the overall evolvement of the knowledge phenomenon aimed at enhancing awareness of the future.

To what extent does objective (physical) reality determine human behavior as opposed to subjective (mental) reality?

Both objective (based on physical reality) needs and psychological (based on subjective reality) needs determine human behavior, which is executed according to a set process sequence.

What accounts for the unity and continuity of experience?

The universality of the process of human behavior accounts for the unity and continuity of experience

Are there knowable universal truths about the world in general or people in particular, or must truth always be relative to an individual or group perspective?

There exist universal truths about the world (at least the one we can comprehend) in general and people in particular, which are not relative to an individual or group perspective. All events and phenomena of the universe (known to us), including the operation of human minds, follow a common process of functioning. The universal truths exist not because humankind possesses superior knowledge or because it is incapable of producing erroneous perceptions. It exists because the human mind is part of the universe and simply cannot conceive anything outside the premise of the universe and outside the uniform process of behavior.

Table 5. *Proposed responses to the persistent questions of psychology.*

	Persistent questions of psychology	Response based on the proposed theory of human behavior
1	What is the nature of human nature?	Human nature is determined by the laws of the preservation of life and the mind. The main principles of human behavior are defined by the process diagram of human behavior (Figure 7).
2	How are the mind and the body related?	The mind emerges from the evolutionary development of the body for the purpose of enhancement of organism preservation. Eventually, the mind becomes so distinguishable that it can be viewed almost as "extrinsic" to the body. Nevertheless, the mind is rooted within the body, affected by the body, and to a large extent controls the body's well-being. The mind often acts in a supervening manner to the body and sometimes negates it by advancing its priorities at the expense of bodily preservation and reproduction. The interrelations between body and mind are both complementary and adversarial as they have separate dominant needs and pursue different priorities in evolutionary development.
3	To what extent are the causes of human behavior innate as opposed to experiential?	The causes of human behavior are both innate and experiential. The proposed theory defines the main steps and factors of the processes of human behavior. It explains interrelations between signals, needs, and experience, and by doing so, provides a platform for further studies and analysis of the innate and experimental causes of behavior.

	Persistent questions of psychology	Response based on the proposed theory of human behavior
4	To what extent, if any, is human behavior freely chosen as opposed to completely determined?	All objects and systems forming the universe known to us are intrinsically reactive. Human behavior is inherently reactive too, i.e., humans react to signals and do so according to a predetermined procedure. The freedom of human behavior originates from the ability to select and influence circumstances generating signals, which they react to. A significant portion of signals triggering behavior is of psychological nature, and in that regard, human behavior is also at least partially determined by an individual.
5	Is there some vital (nonmaterial) force in human nature that prevents a completely mechanistic explanation of human behavior?	The original premise of the new paradigm arises from the materialistic view of human nature. It does not include nonmaterial forces. However, our theory of evolution behavior predicts the possible emergence, and therefore, the possible existence of other forms of nature, which may be perceived as nonmaterial. Hence, though nonmaterial factors are not considered, their possible influence is not entirely discarded.
6	To what extent do the irrational aspects of human nature (for example, emotions, intuitions, and instincts) contribute to human behavior, as opposed to the rational aspects?	The proposed theory does not explicitly address the irrational aspects of human nature as the derived classification of components defining the process of human behavior is relatively high-level. The model provides the basis for further enhancement to account for the role and place of subconsciousness, emotions, etc.

	Persistent questions of psychology	Response based on the proposed theory of human behavior
7	How are humans related to nonhuman animals?	The theory does not distinguish between humans and animals. It approaches the differences between them as quantitative, not qualitative. At one stage, inevitably, quantitative differences transform into new qualities. Has this transformation already happened within the evolution from animals to modern humans? The theory does not give a conclusive answer to this question but provides the basis for further analysis.
8	What is the origin of human knowledge?	Knowledge is the combination of experience and reasoning. The question about the origin of human knowledge must be considered together with another commonly overlooked question: "What is the purpose of human knowledge?" The purpose of knowledge is to facilitate the future orientation of behavior in order to enhance self-preservation. Knowledge is information and as such, is not a unique prerogative of humans or animals but a common feature of animate life and inanimate substances. Human knowledge represents an interim phase in the overall evolvement of the knowledge phenomenon aimed at enhancing awareness of the future.
9	To what extent does objective (physical) reality determine human behavior as opposed to subjective (mental) reality?	Both objective (based on physical reality) needs and psychological (based on subjective reality) needs determine human behavior, which is executed according to a set process sequence.
10	What accounts for the unity and continuity of experience?	The universality of the process of human behavior accounts for the unity and continuity of experience

	Persistent questions of psychology	Response based on the proposed theory of human behavior
11	Are there knowable universal truths about the world in general or people in particular, or must truth always be relative to an individual or group perspective?	There exist universal truths about the world (at least the one we can comprehend) in general and people in particular, which are not relative to an individual or group perspective. All events and phenomena of the universe (known to us), including the operation of human minds, follow a common process of functioning. The universal truths exist not because humankind possesses superior knowledge or because it is incapable of producing erroneous perceptions. It exists because the human mind is part of the universe and simply cannot conceive anything outside the premise of the universe and outside the uniform process of behavior.

The proposed behavioral theory offers new viewpoints on the fundamental questions of psychology and philosophy, particularly those concerning human nature, the relation between body and mind, the relation between humans and nonhuman animals, the unity of experience, and the nature of knowledge (ref. Table 5, items 1, 2, 5, 7, 8, 10, 11). Provided unambiguous responses reflect the ability to uncover the underlying causes of psychological phenomena.

For issues relating to uncovering the origins and intent of human behavior, we explain how the proposed theory can be adapted to address these subjects in further studies (ref. Table 5 items 3, 4, 6, 9).

Afterword

We started with an attempt to apply the basic principles of analytical modeling to psychology by conceptualizing a sDAIRA model of behavior. According to it, a behavioral act consists of a sequence of steps occurring in response to the physical, physiological, psychological, and social type of signals: signal detection(D)-appraisal(A)-intent(I)-risk analysis(R)-act(A). The derived model proved to be a powerful tool that led to the subsequent development of a theory of human happiness, the conceptualization of a dynamic model of human needs, and unified psychology. Eventually, it became evident that issues concerning psychology must be considered together with the matters of philosophy and metaphysics.

Accordingly, we approached behavior and society not as unique features of human living but as fundamental attributes of the universe. We hypothesized that the human psyche evolved as a result of a transition of acts of inanimate matter to the functioning of life and then to the operation of the mind. This transformation occurred through the enhancement of the shared principles of behavior. Consequently, we conceptualized the Law of Universal Behavior. It postulates that the functioning of all elements of the universe, including the human psyche, is governed by a unified set of processes.

Further, we applied similar reasoning to the phenomenon of the congregation and theorized that it developed from material substance to the congregation of organisms and then to culture, i.e., a community of minds. This conceptualization represents a fundamental law of nature in general and psychology in particular – the Law of Congregation.

We argue that all behaviors have a purpose of serving another primary law of nature - the Law of Preservation, which governs the existence of the universe and from which all other laws derive. The origin of the law of preservation is unknown, and its unraveling would equate to answering the question about the meaning of life. For each domain of nature (matter, life, and mind), the law of preservation manifests through more specific postulations, i.e., the preservation of matter, life, and mind. The formulation of the law of preservation of mind complements Darwin's (1859) theory of biological evolution with the theory of the evolvement of the mind.

We linked the law of preservation to the equally comprehensive phenomenon of needs. In this regard, needs are seen not as a uniquely human feature but as a generic attribute of inanimate and animate objects and organisms. It was postulated that the law of preservation manifests itself through a universal need for existence. Subsequently, we conceived a tree of needs according to which the need for existence instigates all other needs, including the basic human needs. The latter are defined as needs upon which the survival of the human species is conditional. The basic needs are elementary, i.e., not composed of other needs, while all other needs originate from them. We consider that the law of preservation of life translates into the basic human needs of self-preservation and reproduction. Also, the law of preservation of mind translates into the basic needs of absorption and dissemination of information. In contrast to conventional theories of motivation, the proposed taxonomy of the four basic needs bridges the science of human behavior to the governing principles of biology and social sciences.

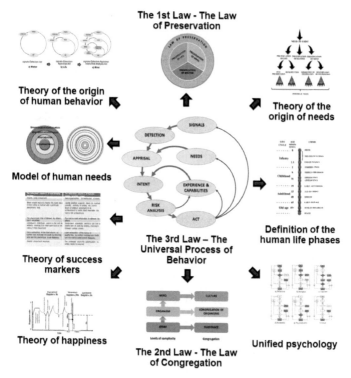

The 1st Law - The Law
of Preservation

Theory of the origin
of human behavior

Theory of the
origin of needs

Model of human needs

Definition of the
human life phases

The 3rd Law – The
Universal Process of
Behavior

Theory of success
markers

Theory of happiness

Unified psychology

The 2nd Law - The Law
of Congregation

Figure 16. Analytical models of the new psychology paradigm.

In their entirety, the proposed models, theories, and laws form a new paradigm of psychology. At the heart of it is the sDAIRA model of human behavior (Figure 16), which gave rise to the diversity of original theories and concepts of diverse psychological phenomena presented in this essay. The multiplicity of the newly derived postulations is an indication of the effectiveness of analytical models applied to social science. Our goal was to position psychology closer to the rank of a "science proper" and to break the spell once cast by Immanuel Kant (1786), who proclaimed that "the empirical doctrine of the soul ... must remain even further ... from the rank of what may be called a natural science proper" (*Preface* 471). We attempt to prove Kant wrong by following his own wisdom: "a doctrine of nature can only contain so much science proper as there is in it of applied mathematics" *(Preface* 470). Thus, we introduce analytical modeling to psychology as an initial step towards advancing the use of "applied mathematics." This is achieved by first defining functional dependencies between components of the human psyche and contemplating grounds for quantitative methods in future psychological research.

Taken together, the proposed theories of the human mind and behavior address the core questions defining a scientific paradigm of psychology:

What is to be observed and scrutinized – Psychology should observe and scrutinize the main components and auxiliary elements of the process of human behavior described in Figure 7.

What kind of questions are supposed to be asked and probed for answers– Psychology should address questions such as: what are the interrelations between the main components of the human behavioral process? What is the structure of these components? How do these components incorporate physical, biological, and mental domains of human nature?

How these questions are to be structured – The questions should inquire about (1) the functional dependences, measurements, and quantification of behavioral processes, (2) how physical, biological, and social processes define psychological phenomena, and (3) how the human psyche shapes social processes.

What predictions are to be made – Psychology should predict (1) human behavior, (2) the future evolutionary development of the human psyche and mind, and (3) the evolvement of social processes using analysis of the human psyche.

We offer a novel unified psychology theory and address many of its persistent questions. Also, we provide a novel interpretation of some essential phenomena of the human psyche, including flow, depression, panic, inner child, the nature of knowledge, the governing social drives of human behavior, the interrelation between body and mind, the behavioral traits of happiness, the future evolution of mind and many others.

On the whole, the newly derived paradigm of psychology and the original concept of metaphysics form an original theory of the meaning of life.

References

Achor, S. (2010). *The happiness advantage: The seven principles of positive psychology that fuel success and performance at work.*

Adamatzky A. (2022). Language of fungi derived from their electrical spiking activity. *R. Soc. Open Sci.* 9: 211926. https://doi.org/10.1098/rsos.211926

Alderfer, C.P. (1969). An empirical test of a new theory of human needs. *Organizational Behavior and Human Performance. 4* (2), 142–75.

American Psychological Association. (n.d.). *APA Dictionary of Psychology.* Retrieved from https://dictionary.apa.org/preparadigmatic-science on May 27, 2022.

Badhwar, N., Long, R. T. (2020). Zalta, Edward N. (ed.). Ayn Rand. Stanford Encyclopedia of Philosophy. Archived from the original on March 24, 2022. Retrieved on May 3, 2021.

Baker, L. (2023, January 23). *What is The 'Ant Death Spiral', and Why Do They Do It?* AZ Animals. https://a-z-animals.com/blog/what-is-the-ant-death-spiral-and-why-do-they-do-it/

Bechtereva, N.P. Ed. (1988). *Mechanisms of human brain function. Part one.* Human neurophysiology. Leningrad: Nauka. Russian ed.

Bostrom, N. (2014.). *Superintelligence: Paths, Dangers, Strategies.* Oxford University Press.

Boyd, J.R. (1987). *Destruction and Creation.* U.S. Army Command and General Staff College.

Bradburn, N. (1969). *The structure of psychological well-being.* Aldine.

Bruineberg, J., Kiverstein, J., Rietveld, E. (2018). The anticipating brain is not a scientist: The free-energy principle from an ecological-enactive perspective. *Synthese. 195*, 2417–2444. https://doi.org/10.1007/s11229-016-1239-1

Bureau of Labor Statistics. (2022, April 18). *Occupational Outlook Handbook, Psychologists*, BLS. Retrieved from https://www.bls.gov/ooh/life-physical-and-social-science/psychologists.htm

Caesar, M. (1999). *Umberto Eco: Philosophy, Semiotics, and the Work of Fiction*. Wiley-Blackwell. p. 55. ISBN 978-0-7456-0850-1.

Calhoun, J. B. (1970). Population density and social pathology. *California Medicine. 113* (5): 54. PMC 1501789. PMID 18730425.

Calhoun, J. B. (1973). Death squared: The explosive growth and demise of a mouse population. *Proceedings of the Royal Society of Medicine. 66* (1 Pt 2): 80–88. doi:10.1177/00359157730661P202. PMC 1644264. PMID 4734760

Coppola, F. (2019) The brain in solitude: an (other) eighth amendment challenge to solitary confinement. *Journal of Law and the Biosciences. 6* (1): 184–225. https://doi.org/10.1093/jlb/lsz014

Cronbach, L. J. (1957). The two disciplines of scientific psychology. *American Psychologist, 12*, 671-684.

Csikszentmihalyi, M. (1975). *Beyond boredom and anxiety*. Jossey-Bass.

Csikszentmihalyi, M. (1990). *Flow: The psychology of optimal experience*. Harper and Row. ISBN 0-06-092043-2

Csikszentmihalyi, M. (2002). *Flow: The Classic work on how to achieve happiness*. Rider Books.

Cummins, R. (2010). Subjective wellbeing, homeostatically protected mood and depression: A Synthesis. *Journal of Happiness Studies, 11*, 1–17. http://dx.doi.org/10.1007/s10902-009-9167-0

Darwin, C. R. (1859). *On the origin of species*. Murray.

Darwin, C. R. (1871). *The Descent of Man, and Selection in Relation to Sex*. John Murray.

D'Alessio, M., Guarino, A., DePascalis, V., Zimbardo, P.G. (2003). Testing Zimbardo's Stanford Time Perspective Inventory

(STPI) -Short Form, *Time & Society*; *Vol. 12* No. 2/3, pp. 333–347 0961-463X[200309]12:2/3;333–347;032375

Davidson, R.J., Schuyler, B.S. (2015). Neuroscience of happiness. *World happiness report*. The earth institute, Columbia University; 88-105.

Denes-Raj, V., Epstein, S. (1994). Conflict between intuitive and rational processing: When people behave against their better judgment. *Journal of Personality and Social Psychology; 66*, 819–829.

Diener, E. (1984). Subjective well-being. *Psychological Bulletin, 95*, 542-575.

Diener, E. (2013). The remarkable changes in the science of subjective well-being. *Perspectives on Psychological Science, 8*(6), 663-666

Diener, E., Suh, E.M., Lucas, R.E., Smith, H.L. (1999) Subjective Well-Being: Three Decades of Progress. *Psychological Bulletin*; *Vol. 125*, No. 2, 276-302.

Diener, E., Oishi, S., Lucas, R.E. (2002). Subjective well-being: The science of happiness and life satisfaction. In Snyder CR, Lopez SJ. Eds., *Handbook of Positive Psychology*. Oxford University Press.

Diener, E., Sandvik, E., Pavot, W. (2009). Happiness is the frequency, not the intensity, of positive versus negative affect. *In Assessing well-being* (pp. 213-231). Springer Netherlands.

Diener, E., Biswas-Diener, R. (2020). The replication crisis in psychology. In R. Biswas-Diener & E. Diener (Eds), Noba textbook series: Psychology. Champaign, IL: DEF publishers. Retrieved from http://noba.to/q4cvydeh.

Dodge, R., Daly, A., Huyton, J., Sanders, L. (2012). The challenge of defining wellbeing. *International Journal of Wellbeing, 2*(3), 222-235. doi:10.5502/ijw.v2i3.4.

Dorigo, M. (1992). Optimization, Learning and Natural Algorithms, PhD thesis, Politecnico di Milano, Italy.

Epstein, S. (1994). Integration of the cognitive and the psychodynamic unconscious. *American Psychologist* 1994; *49*, 709–724.

Erikson, E.H., Erikson, J.M. (1998). The Life Cycle Completed: Extended Version (W. W. Norton, 1998.

Forgeard, M.J.C., Jayawickreme, E., Kern, M., Seligman, M.E.P. (2011). Doing the right thing: Measuring wellbeing for public policy. *International Journal of Wellbeing*; *1*(1), 79–106. http://dx.doi.org/10.5502/ijw.v1i1.15

Freeman, S., Herron, J.C. (2004). *Evolutionary Analysis* (3rd ed.). Upper Saddle River, NJ: Pearson Education. ISBN 978-0-13-101859-4. LCCN 2003054833. OCLC 52386174

Freud, S. (1933). *New introductory lectures on psychoanalysis.* In Strachey J. (Ed. & Trans.), *The complete psychological works* (Vol. 16). Norton 1976

Friston, K.J. (2010). The free-energy principle: a unified brain theory? *Nature Reviews, Neuroscience, 11*(2): 127-38.

Galperin, P.J. (1976). *Introduction to psychology.* Russian ed.

Garnett, C. (2008). Plumbing the "Behavioral Sink", Medical Historian Examines NIMH Experiments in Crowding. Archived 2020-08-15 at the Wayback Machine. NIH Record. Retrieved on July 7, 2013.

Gawdat, M. (2019). *Solve for happy: engineer your path to joy.* Bluebird

Gilbert, D. (2006). *Stumbling on happiness.* Alfred A. Knopf

Goff, P. (2019). *Galileo's Error: Foundations for a New Science of Consciousness.* Vintage, Pantheon. ISBN 0525564772.).

Green, C. D. (2015). Why psychology isn't unified, and probably never will be. *Review of General Psychology, 19*, No. 3, 207–214. Retrieved from http://dx.doi.org/10.1037/gpr0000051

Guyer, P., Horstmann, R.P. (2019). Idealism, in Zalta, Edward N. (ed.), *The Stanford Encyclopedia of Philosophy* (Winter 2019 ed.), Metaphysics Research Lab, Stanford University. Retrieved on January 22, 2020

Harari, Yuval N. author. (2015). *Sapiens: a brief history of humankind.* Harper

Hayes, S. C. (2004). Taxonomy as a contextualist views it. *Journal of Clinical Psychology, 60,* 1231–1235. doi:10.1002/jclp.20064

Hawking, S. (1988). *A brief history of time*. Bantam Books. ISBN 978-0-553-38016-3

Hawking, S., Redmayne, E., Thorne, K. S., & Hawking, L. (2018). *Brief answers to the big questions*. John Murray.

Headey, B., Wearing, A. (1992). *Understanding happiness: A theory of subjective well-being*. Longman Cheshire.

Helliwell, J., Layard, R., Sachs, J., Eds. (2015). *World Happiness Report 2015*. Sustainable Development Solutions Network.

Helliwell, J., Layard, R., Sachs, J., Eds. (2017). *World Happiness Report*, Sustainable Development Solutions Network 2017.

Henriques, G. (2003). The Tree of Knowledge System and the Theoretical Unification of Psychology. *Review of General Psychology*, *7*(2):150-182.

Henriques, G. (2011). *A new unified theory of psychology*. Springer.

Henriques, G., Michalski, J. (2020.) Defining Behavior and its Relationship to the Science of *Psychology. Integr. psych. behav. 54,* 328–353. https://doi.org/10.1007/s12124-019-09504-4

Henriques, G., Michalski, J., Quackenbush, S., Schmidt, W. (2019). The Tree of Knowledge System: A New Map for Big History. *Journal of Big History*, *3*(4); 1 - 17. DOI https://doi.org/10.22339/jbh.v3i4.3410

Hergenhahn, B.R. (2008). *An Introduction to the History of Psychology*. Cengage Learning.

Hollis, J. (1993). *The middle passage: From misery to meaning in midlife*. Inner City Books.

ISO 45001 Occupational health and safety". www.iso.org. Retrieved 13 March 2018.

Jebb, D., Huang, Z., Pippel, M. et al. (2020). Six reference-quality genomes reveal the evolution of bat adaptations. Nature *583*, 578–584. https://doi.org/10.1038/s41586-020-2486-3

Kant, I. (1786). The Metaphysical Foundations of Natural Science. Tr. Ernest Belfort Bax 1883.

Kenrik, D.T., Griskevicius, V., Neuberg, S.L., Schaller, M. (2010). Renovating the pyramid of needs: contemporary extensions built upon ancient foundations. *Perspectives on*

Psychological Science; May; *5*(3): 292-314. Doi: 10.117771745691610369469

Killingsworth, M.A., Gilbert, D.T. (2010). A wandering mind is an unhappy mind. *Science*; *330*(6006), 932. doi:10.1126/science.1192439

Kimble, G. A. (1996). *Psychology: The hope of a science.* MIT Press.

Kirchhoff, M., Froese, T. (2017). Where there is life there is mind: In support of a strong life-mind continuity thesis. *Entropy*, *19*(4), e19040169-1-e19040169-18.

Kolarik, A. J., Cirstea, S., Pardhan, S., Moore, B.C.J. (2014). A summary of research investigating echolocation abilities of blind and sighted humans. *Hearing Research, 310*: 60–68. doi:10.1016/j.heares.2014.01.010)

Kopsov, I. (2019a). A new model of subjective well-being. *The Open Psychology Journal*, *12*(1):102-115.

Kopsov, I. (2019b). A new model of human needs. *London Journal of Research in Science: Natural and Formal*, *19*(6), 17-28.

Kopsov, I. (2020a). It's time for psychology to become a (great) science. *Curr Res Psychol Behav Sci.*, *1*(3): 1011.

Kopsov, I. (2020b). On the origin of human behavior. *Sage Submissions.* Preprint. https://doi.org/10.31124/advance.12151791.v1

Kopsov, I. (2021a). Comparison of algorithms of individual and group behavior. *Advances in Social Sciences Research Journal, 8*(2):487-510 DOI: 10.14738/assrj.82.9750.

Kopsov, I. (2021b). A new model of unified psychology. *Advances in Social Sciences Research Journal 8*(3):363-384 DOI: 10.14738/assrj.83.9884

Kopsov, I. (2021c). A new theory of human behavior and motivation. *Advances in Social Sciences Research Journal 8*(10): 345-364.DOI: 10.14738/assrj.810.11088

Korotayev, A. (2018). The 21st Century Singularity and its Big History Implications: A re-analysis. *Journal of Big History 2*(3): 74-120. https://doi.org/10.22339/jbh.v2i3.2329

Kurzweil, R. (2005). *The singularity is near: When humans transcend biology.* Penguin.

Levinson, D.J. (1986). A conception of adult development. *American Psychologist.* 41:3–13. doi:10.1037/0003-066X.41.1.3.

Lilienfeld S.O., Arkowitz H. (2012) Are All Psychotherapies Created Equal? Scientific American Mind *23*(4), 68-69 (September 2012), doi:10.1038/scientificamericanmind0912-68

Loeb, A (2021). Was our universe created in a laboratory? *Scientific American*, October 15, 2021.

Lotman, Y.M. (1990). *Universe of the Mind: A Semiotic Theory of Culture.* (Translated by Ann Shukman, introduction by Umberto Eco.) I. B. Tauris & Co Ltd. xiii+288 p. ISBN 978-1-85043-375-0

Lyubomirsky, S. (2011). Hedonic adaptation to positive and negative experiences. In Folkman S. Ed., *The Oxford handbook of stress, health, and coping.* Oxford University Press, pp. 200-224.

Lu, L. (2001). Understanding happiness: A look into the Chinese folk psychology. *Journal of Happiness*, *2*(4), 407–432.

Luthans, F., & Davis, T. (1979). Behavioral self-management—The missing link in managerial effectiveness. *Organizational Dynamics*, *8*(1):42-60.

Malthus, T.R. (1798). *An essay on the principle of population as it affects the future improvement of society, with remarks on the speculations of Mr. Goodwin, M. Condorcet and other writers (1 ed.)* J. Johnson. (Anonymous publication)

Maslow, A.H. (1943a) A preface to motivation theory. *Psychosomatic Med.* 1943; 5, 85-92.

Maslow, A.H. (1943b). A theory of human motivation. *Psychological Review.* *50*(4): 370–96.

Maslow, A. H. (1970a). *Motivation and personality.* Harper & Row.

Maslow, A. H. (1970b). *Religions, values, and peak experiences.* Penguin. (Original work published 1966)

McKay, C. (2014, September 18). What is life? It's a Tricky, Often Confusing Question. *Astrobiology Magazine*

Mehrabian, A. (1981). *Silent Messages: Implicit Communication of Emotions and Attitudes* (2nd ed.). Belmont, CA: Wadsworth. ISBN 0-534-00910-7.

Munch E. MM T 2547, Munchmuseet. Datert 1930–1935. Skissebok. Page 59 https://emunch.no/HYBRIDNo-MM_T2547.xhtml

Murray, H. A. (1938). *Explorations in personality*. Oxford University Press.

McClelland, D. (1988). *Human motivation*. Cambridge University Press.

McMahon, D. M. (2006). *Happiness: A history*. Atlantic Monthly Press.

Nagel, T. (1974). What is it like to be a bat?". *The Philosophical Review. 83* (4): 435–450. doi:10.2307/2183914. JSTOR 2183914.

Norcross, J. C. (2005). A primer on psychotherapy integration. In J. C. Norcross & M. R. Goldfried (Eds.), *Handbook of psychotherapy integration* (pp. 3–23). Oxford Press.

Norcross, J. C., & Goldfried, M. R. (Eds.). (2005). *Oxford series in clinical psychology. Handbook of psychotherapy integration (2nded.)*. Oxford University Press.

OECD (2013). *OECD Guidelines on measuring subjective well-being*, OECD Publishing-

Oishi, S., Graham, J., Kesebir, S., Galinha, I.C. (2013). Concepts of Happiness Across Time and Cultures. *Personality and Social Psychology Bulletin, 39*(5), 559-577. First Published April 18.

Orben, A., Lucas, R.E., Fuhrmann, D., Kievit, R.A. (2022). Trajectories of adolescent life satisfaction. *R. Soc. Open Sci.* 9: 211808. https://doi.org/10.1098/rsos.211808

Pavlov, I. (2010). Conditioned reflexes: An investigation of the physiological activity of the cerebral cortex. *Annals of neurosciences, 17*(3):136–141.

Rand, A. (1995) [1938]. Anthem. Introduction and appendix by Leonard Peikoff (50th anniversary ed.) Dutton. ISBN 0-525-94015-4

Ramsey, F.P. (2001). Truth and Probability. Chapter VII in *The Foundations of Mathematics and other Logical Essays*, Reprinted, Routledge 1931; ISBN 0-415-22546-9.

Reiss, S. (2004). The 16 strivings for God. *Zygon, 39*, 303-320.

Robinson-Riegler, B., Robinson-Riegler, G. (2012). *Cognitive Psychology: Applying the Science of the Mind* (Third ed.). Boston, MA: Pearson Education Inc. as Allyn & Bacon. pp. 272–276, 295–296, 339–346. ISBN 978-0-205-17674-8.

Roser, M., Ortiz-Ospina, E., Ritchie, H. (2013). Life Expectancy. Published online at OurWorldInData.org. Retrieved from: https://ourworldindata.org/life-expectancy

Rutledge, R.B., Skandali, N., Dayan, P., Dolan, R.J. (2014). A computational and neural model of momentary subjective well-being. *Proc. Natl Acad. Sci. USA*; 111, 12252–12257

Rutledge, R.B, de Berker, A.O., Espenhahn, S., Dayan, P., Dolan, RJ. (2016). The social contingency of momentary subjective well-being. *Nat. Commun;* 7:11825 doi: 10.1038/ncomms11825.

Rutherford, A. (2020). *The book of humans: a brief history of culture, sex, war, and the evolution of us*, 256 Pages, Published 2020 by The Experiment ISBN: 978-1-61519-590-9

Savage, L.J. (1954). *The Foundations of Statistics.* Wiley.

Sawyer, S.M., Azzopardi, P.S., Wickremarathne, D, Patton, G.C. (2018). The age of adolescence. *Lancet Child Adolesc. Health 2*, 223–228. (doi: 10.1016/ S2352-4642(18)30022-1

Schuyler, B.S., Kral, T.R.A., Jacquart, J., Burghy, C.A., Weng, H.Y., Perlman, D.M., Davidson, R.J. (2012). Temporal dynamics of emotional responding: Amygdala recovery predicts emotional traits. *Social Cognitive and Affective Neuroscience*; doi:10.1093/scan/nss131.

Schwarz, N., Strack, F. (1991). Evaluating one's life: A judgment model of subjective well-being. In Strack F, Argyle M, Schwarz N. Eds., *Subjective well-being: An interdisciplinary perspective* (pp. 27-47). Pergamon.

Seligman, M.E., Csikszentmihalyi, M. (2000). Positive Psychology: An introduction. *American Psychologist, 55* (1): 5–14. doi:10.1037/0003-066x.55.1.5.

Seligman, M.E. (2012). *Flourish: A visionary new understanding of happiness and well-being.* Simon and Schuster.

Sellars, R.W. (1926). *The principles and problems of philosophy.* Macmillan.

Sheldon, K.M., Lyubomirsky, S. (2007). Is it possible to become happier? (And, if so, how?) *Social and Personality Psychology* Compass, 1, 129–145.

Shin, D., Johnson, D. (1978). Avowed happiness as an overall assessment of the quality of life. *Social Indicators Research*; 5(1), 475–492.http://dx.doi.org/10.1007/BF00352944

Sternberg, R. J., Grigorenko, E. L. (2001). Unified psychology. *American Psychologist*, 56, 1069–1079.

Stutzer, A., Frey, B.S. (2006). Does marriage make people happy, or do happy people get married? *The Journal of Socio-Economics*; 35. 326–347.

Tay, L., Diener, E. (2011). Needs and subjective well-being around the world. Journal of Personality and Social Psychology, 101(2), 354–365. doi: 10.1037/a0023779

Thorndike, E. (1898). Animal Intelligence: An Experimental Study of the Associative Processes in Animals. *Psychological Review*, 5(5):551-553.

UN General Assembly Resolution A/65/L.86 (13 July 2011).

Varela, F. J., Thompson, E., & Rosch, E. (1991). *The embodied mind: Cognitive science and human experience*, MIT press.

Vazza, F., Feletti, A. (2020). The Quantitative Comparison Between the Neuronal Network and the Cosmic Web. Front. Phys. 8:525731. doi: 10.3389/fphy.2020.525731

Veenhoven, R. (2009). How Do We Assess How Happy We Are? Tenets, Implications and Tenability of Three Theories. In Dutt, A. K. & Radcliff, B. (Eds.) *Happiness, economics and politics: Towards a multi-disciplinary approach*. Edward Elger Publishers, Cheltenham UK, Chapter 3, 45–69.

Volkov, A. G., Carrell, H., Baldwin, A., Markin, V. S. (2009). Electrical memory in Venus flytrap. *Bioelectrochemistry. 75* (2): 142–147. doi:10.1016/j.bioelechem.2009.03.005. PMID 19356999

Von Neumann, J., & Morgenstern, O. (2007). Theory of games and economic behavior. In *Theory of games and economic behavior*. Princeton university press.

Wallace, A.R. (1858). On the tendency of varieties to depart indefinitely from the original type. *Journal of the Proceedings of the Linnean Society: Zoology*, 3(9), 53-62.

Wampold, B.E. (2001). *The great psychotherapy debate: models, methods, and findings*. Routledge.

Webster's Third New International Dictionary of the English Language by Philip Babcock Gove Hardcover (Editor).

Weisberger, M. (2019, February 15). *Reindeer Cyclones Are Real, and You Definitely Don't Want to Get Caught in One.* Livescience. https://www.livescience.com/64778-vikings-reindeer-cyclone.html

Wierzbicka, A. (1999). *Emotions Across Languages and Cultures: Diversity and Universals*. Cambridge University Press.

Wierzbicka, A. (2004). Happiness in cross-linguistic & cross-cultural perspective, *Daedalus*, V133(2), 34-43. doi: 10.1162/001152604323049370

Wilber, K. (2001). *A theory of everything: An integral vision for business, politics, science, and spirituality*. Shambhala.

Wilson, E. O. (1998). *Consilience: The unity of knowledge*. Alfred A. Knopf, Inc

Wilson, T.D., Gilbert, D.N. (2003). Affective forecasting. *Advances in experimental social psychology, 35*. 345-411.

Wilson, W. (1967) Correlates of avowed happiness. *Psychological Bulletin*; 67, 294-306.

White, R. (2022, November 21). *Mystery of Sheep Walking in Circle in China for 12 Days Potentially Solved.* Newsweek. https://www.newsweek.com/mystery-sheep-circle-china-12-days-potentially-solved-1760985

Whitehead, A.N. (1985) *Symbolism: Its meaning and effect*, Fordham University Press.

Woodworth, R.S. (1918). *Dynamic Psychology*. Columbia University Press.

Zimbardo, P.G., Boyd, J.N. (1999). Putting Time in Perspective: A Valid, Reliable Individual-Differences Metric, *Journal of Personality and Social Psychology*; 77: 1271–88.

About the Author

Engineer with a Ph.D. Igor Kopsov lives in Norway and is the proud father of two adult children. He works in the energy sector, overseeing the engineering of some of the world's most complex industrial systems. In recent years he has acquired an interest in psychology. He is an author of papers on human behavior and a speaker at leading psychological conferences. He employs an engineering approach and analytical modeling to the most fundamental topics of psychology and philosophy, including humankind's origin and future evolution, the pursuit of happiness, and the meaning of life. Using his background in applied sciences, he views social disciplines as requiring a solution-focused mindset, rational attitude, and innovative ways of thinking.

Printed in Great Britain
by Amazon